From Fish to Glory

©2020, Robert C. Beasley

ISBN: 978-1-09834-370-5
ISBN eBook: 978-1-09834-371-2

1 PETER FOR DAILY LIVING

From

Fish

to

Glory

ROBERT C. BEASLEY

TABLE OF CONTENTS

FROM FISH TO GLORY

There once was a man whose life was a daily grind. Every day, it was the same routine: Get up, go to work, come home, eat, visit family, go to bed. Next morning: Get up, go to work, come back, eat, visit family, go to bed. On his way to work one morning, he thought to himself:

"This job stinks! It's the same thing, day in, day out. By noon I'm knee-deep in muck. Sometimes I put out the bait for more work, but I never get a nibble. Sometimes I feel like I'm in over my head, and the water's coming in faster than I can bail it out. Sometimes I just feel like I'm sinking. This job stinks!"

Ever feel like that?

You're tired of your job. The daily grind grinds you down. The routine is boring. Maybe you feel like this guy. Shouldn't there be more to life?

This man's job was similar in many ways to jobs we might have, but it was also slightly different. His job did stink. Literally, it *stunk*.

This man was a fisherman, and his job stunk. The fish stunk; his hands stunk; his clothes reeked. Many times he was knee-deep in mud. There were times when he was bailing water as fast as it was coming in. Sometimes, he sat all day and didn't bring a thing home to eat. Like you and me, he probably got tired of the daily grind, wondering if there was "more" to life than fishing for a living.

And then he came face to face with GLORY, and nothing was ever the same.

This man's work went from fishing for a living to fishing for people. His life went from daily grind to divine glory. His purpose went from making a living to living for his Maker.

The best way he could describe this new perspective was "GLORY!" The light was breaking in and illuminating every aspect of his life, even the daily grind. As he put it, life was filled with an "inexpressible and glorious joy."

What brought about this change?

He had a very close encounter of the Divine Kind. He came face to face with the God of the Universe, and that God turned out to be none other than *his best friend*!

The man I'm talking about is Simon Peter, and his best friend is Jesus of Nazareth, who was raised from the dead. (By the way, this Jesus is still alive and roaming the world. He has shaped the course of culture for the last 2,000 years. He will continue to triumph over culture and within history until he finally prevails over every evil force in the universe, including death itself).

So is your life boring? Is the daily grind getting you down? Maybe life has been difficult, and suffering has knocked the hope out of you. Let me assure you: there is hope in this universe. Life undergoes a complete turnaround when you meet someone who has come back from the dead!

From Fish to Glory

History tells us that this one Simon from Galilee went from an illiterate fisherman to the leader of the most significant cultural revolution ever. Parents began naming their kids after him. Billions of people over two millennia have been impacted by his teachings and work. His picture is painted in the greatest museums in the world. The greatest of all churches, St. Peter's Basilica in Rome, is named after him. Peter went from fisherman to fame. But please don't think he found his glory in fame. Fame, money, or pleasure was not where he found real glory.

He would tell you that his life went from grind to glory when the God of the universe broke into his life and stole his heart, his work, his purpose. He would describe his transformation much like a seed that takes root and grows supernaturally beyond your wildest dreams. He would describe it as a second chance, a "new birth," the reality of living life to the full.

For him, "new birth" wasn't religious jargon. He had been religious for years. What he was talking about was an intimate encounter with God, allowing God to have control of all of his life's ambitions and desires. He now had HOPE, the greatest of all hopes, the hope of continuous and ever-increasing glory and purpose and a life with ever-increasing love. He would describe this hope as a "living thing," a "living hope" that gets more and more sure the longer you live. This hope is that we will live forever in love and never die. This hope tells us that everything we do in life can have eternal meaning and purpose. Most people start losing hope as they get older; Peter's hope grew more robust and confident as he aged.

Peter had known this hope close up. Like his fishing buddy John, he had seen this glory and hope with his own eyes. He had touched this hope with his own hands. He had looked into the eyes of One who had risen from the dead. And even more than that, he had felt the embrace of his best friend, risen from the dead. Nothing was ever the same again.

The Writings of a Rascal

But this kind of hope is not just for Peter or for those who saw the risen Jesus face to face. You and I can know this same glory and hope, too. To help us encounter the risen Jesus, Peter wrote two books: 1 and 2 Peter. I would argue that these books are the *most amazing, and the most import-ant, books ever written.* How can I make this claim?

First, they are written by someone who could claim to be the best friend of the Son of God. They are written by a man who was part of the intimate circle of God in the flesh. He saw with his own eyes the risen Jesus. Have you ever seen anyone rise from the dead? I haven't either. But you can bet that if I ever did encounter someone who had been raised from the dead, I would certainly listen to them, wouldn't you? Peter and John were probably Jesus' best friends, and Jesus spoke directly to them. Whatever Peter wants to tell us, we should listen.

Second, they are written by an ordinary working stiff like you and me. Peter wasn't a scholar by any means. He was a blue-collar worker. You and I are highly educated compared to Peter. But it is incredible how God uses ordinary folks in glorious ways. Peter would tell us that there are no ordinary people in God's eyes. Instead, we are all "chosen" and "precious" to God. We are all "priests" to Him, and we are destined for glorious things.

Finally, and most importantly, these books were written by a rascal. When Jesus first laid eyes on Peter, Peter was no saint. He was boister-ous, brash, crude, and cocky. He was impatient, impetuous, immature, and immoral. He was a windbag and wishy-washy. *He was just the kind of guy God chooses!* And he was just the kind of guy God *changes.* Peter was, in his own words, a "sinful man," and I can relate to that. If there is hope for proud Peter, there is hope for you and me. Jesus took him right where he was and slowly, patiently, and lovingly changed him.

When Jesus found Peter, his name was "Simon," which was a com-mon Jewish name. Jesus gave him a new identity and began calling him by a new name, Peter, which means "Rock." Jesus loved him not only for who he was but for who Jesus was going to transform him into being. Jesus never stopped loving him even though Peter would fail him time and again.

I love Peter because I am so much like him. I can identify with him, as maybe you can, too. What I like about Peter is that he is proof that God will not abandon a sinner who fails time and again, but will make sure His glorious purposes win out. That is *good news!*

The Three Most Important Questions

My purpose is to take an in-depth look at Peter's first book to learn the lessons God wants to teach us for everyday living. 1 Peter is a perfect book for this because it answers the three most essential questions in life:

- *What is life for?*

- *What do we do with suffering?*

- *How do we live?*

You need to read through 1 Peter (preferably in one sitting) to find Peter's answers, but here is a sneak preview:

1. What is life for?

In a word, GLORY! The term "glory" fills Peter's thoughts. The word for glory (*doxa*) and its corresponding verb (*doxazein*) appear 13 times in 1 Peter, more than in any other New Testament book! Peter caught a glimpse of true glory when he saw the white, glowing face of Jesus on Mount Hermon at Jesus' "transfiguration," and when he saw the risen Jesus, alive again from the dead. He caught a glimpse of supernatural glory, and anything less than that was boring.

But Jesus went away. The risen Jesus, his best friend, disappeared into the heavens, and he would never see him face to face again on this earth. Jesus was no longer around to touch, to talk to, to cry with, to joke with. Did the glory stop?

Peter discovered that after Jesus left, the glory had just begun! What is life for? Life is for God's glory and our involvement in that glory. Peter makes it clear from the first that God has deliberately chosen every one of us for a unique, divine purpose. Like Peter, God calls us to follow him into a life filled with glory, adventure, and ever-increasing meaning.

Peter tells us we have to choose how we view life. We can see life either as a series of meaningless routines or as a daily adventure. We can choose to view life as all about work, or we can view life as all about ever-in-creasing glory. We can see ourselves as fishers of fish for a living or living to "fish" for people.

I'm not saying that every day will be full of heart-thumping adventure where we're raising people from the dead, casting out evil spirits, and healing sick people. When I read 1 Peter, I don't see those things as being the "adventure" that Peter is talking about. The adventure is instead risking your life by "betting" it on God. The adventure is entrusting your life to the God of the Universe and *slowly* seeing the harvest of joy, love, character, and lasting heritage. The adventure is trusting God even in suffering and seeing Him turn suffering into glory, just like he did with the cross of Jesus. The adventure is realizing that it is when you lose your life for the sake of Jesus that you end up finding it! Peter says the daily grind itself can become the resting place of the Presence of God, filling even ordinary jobs with eternal meaning and purpose. This is the choice we must make.

It was the same choice Jesus gave to Peter on the Sea of Galilee. If you remember, Jesus met Peter at a very vulnerable time in Peter's life. Remember the scene (Luke 5:1-11)? Peter and his buddies had been fishing all night. They weren't fishing for fun, either. Fishing was Peter's livelihood. Peter's family depended on Peter's catch of fish. And all night long, he hadn't caught a single snapper, not one little fish. Peter was dead tired, ready to go home to tell his wife the bad news and get some much-needed sleep.

At that vulnerable point, Jesus challenged him: "Set out your nets a little *deeper.*"

What? Are you crazy? Peter might have been thinking, "I don't need a carpenter to tell me how to fish! And why go deeper? That will require me to go back out into the sea, making an effort that seems useless." I don't know why Peter did it (maybe it was to prove that Jesus was crazy), but he took Jesus' bait (no pun intended), rowed out into deeper water, and let his nets down.

What Peter saw next could only be described as "Glory!" Peter's fishing nets were overflowing with fish! Imagine the scene: scales gleaming in the sunlight, fins and flippers flying everywhere, water splashing, nets breaking, people yelling. Peter could not believe his eyes. He was thrilled and astonished.

And humbled. He quickly realized a Master had outmaneuvered him. He had come up against Someone he couldn't control or figure out. He immediately said, "Depart from me, Jesus, for I am a sinful man" (Luke 5:8).

The question we need to ask ourselves is this: Why did Jesus do this miracle? Did Jesus perform the miracle so Peter could buy a new house with the extra cash he'd get from the fish? Or maybe a new boat? Or perhaps so Peter could use Jesus' power to acquire money, fame, and fortune?

Question: What was Jesus trying to teach Peter by performing this incredible miracle?

Answer: The same thing he's trying to teach all of us working stiffs: If you trust Jesus with the material stuff, He will lead you on to greater things in the one area of life that matters, your *soul*.

God showed Peter a miracle in his material life to prove that he could be trusted in spiritual things. God may do miraculous things in our lives not just to give us a glimpse of what He can do, but more importantly, to move us from trusting in material things (and trusting in ourselves) to trusting all of our life to him. That is why sometimes it's not the "miraculous" that God uses to teach us trust, but suffering (more on this below).

What is life for? It's not just to catch fish for a living. It's not only to make money, or pay bills, or spend money, or whatever else that makes up the routine ruts of life. Jesus told Peter, "From now on, you will be catching people" (Luke 5:10). Jesus turns our perspective from being "Me" centered to being "You" centered, from an entirely selfish outlook on the universe to one that resembles the heart of God reflected in Jesus Christ. Life is for loving people. Life is for impacting people. Life is for relationships. Life is for loving others with selfless love and seeing them, in turn, grow into loving and giving people. Life is for catching people, for going on the great adventures God has designed for us.

2. What do we do with suffering?

Peter was an eye-witness to the most unfair suffering the world has ever seen: The wrongful crucifixion of the most innocent of men. But that was just the beginning. Peter himself was acquainted with suffering, much of which also may be familiar to you:

The suffering of lost dreams: Peter denied knowing Jesus three times. Why would he deny his best friend? It might have been because he was scared. But I think the real reason was that he was *discouraged.* His dreams of glory were going down the tubes. The grand vision he had about Jesus (that Jesus would triumphantly rescue Israel from the Romans) was crashing down. It was dawning on him that Jesus was going to prison or worse. I'm sure Peter was thinking: "Is this worth it anymore?"

Have you ever felt like that? Have you ever realized that one of your dreams in life was just a pipe dream? Have you ever been betrayed by a friend, or dumped by a lover? Have you lost someone you loved deeply? Have you lost a job or lost your self-esteem or confidence? What do we do at times like these?

The suffering of failure: When Peter denied Jesus, Peter suffered doubly. Not only was it the suffering of lost dreams, but it was also the suffering of failure. He had wholly denied the One he loved. Hours before, he had proudly announced (with his cocky attitude) that he would go to his death for Jesus. Now he had denied ever knowing him (with curse words, too). He had let his best friends down! Have you ever done that? Would you say you are completely satisfied with the way you have lived your life? Do you feel the tinge of suffering when you think back on the memories of your greatest failures? When you're alone, do the haunting sounds of "if only" whisper in your ear? What do we do at times like these?

Unjust suffering: 1 Peter deals a lot with the kind of suffering that is particularly difficult: "unjust suffering." Peter distinguishes between two types of suffering we experience in life: suffering that comes because of our own actions or decisions; and suffering that comes unexpectedly and is unfair or unjust. Peter says that if you suffer, it should not be because of your bad decisions or bad behavior (1 Peter 4:15; 3:17). Although any kind of suffering is painful, unjust suffering is often the most painful because it seems so meaningless. You may have experienced some of these questions in life: "Why did I have to get this disease?" "Why did she have to die so young?" "Why was I the one picked for this difficult job—it's unfair!?" "Why this, why me, why now?" The words "Why" and "Unfair!" seem to go hand in hand.

Peter also knew unjust suffering. Soon after he began telling people about the resurrection of Jesus, he was imprisoned and flogged numerous times by the authorities (Acts 5:40). Throughout his ministry, Peter faced intense persecution. Tradition says that Peter and his wife were crucified in Rome on the same day. Peter chose to be crucified upside down because he did not feel worthy of being executed in the same manner as his risen Lord. Peter, like Paul, suffered unjustly in all kinds of "hardships and distresses; in beatings, imprisonments and riots; in hard work, sleepless nights and hunger" (2 Corinthians 6:4-5).

The first recipients of 1 Peter were also facing persecution and unjust suffering. Peter experienced and witnessed daily the unjust suffering that Christians endure. Peter's decision to continue to endure such persecution in his life (and ultimately face an excruciating death) proves the reality of the risen Lord in his life. If Peter, who claimed to be an eyewitness to the resurrection, were making it all up, then he would not have allowed himself such persecution. But he wasn't making it up. Not only was he an eyewitness to the resurrection of Jesus, but he was also a witness of the sufferings of Jesus (1 Peter 5:1). Peter saw that God Himself, in the form of Jesus, also suffered unjustly.

So what do we do with Suffering?

Suffering. Evil. Pain. None of these makes life easy. They all make our understanding of God difficult. Why does God allow suffering? Although Peter, the one who was crucified upside down, doesn't answer all of our questions, he does give us some helpful answers:

Suffering can purify us. If you only had a few months to live, would you live differently? Suffering and death make us view life from a different perspective. Suffering also can have a way of "purifying" our character, making us more compassionate toward and patient with others. Suffering enables us to take a "long" view of life. Just like metal is refined in the fire, so this "veil of tears" can have a purifying effect on our souls. Peter tells the churches to whom he is writing that their unjust suffering has come "so that your faith, of greater worth than gold, which is perishable even though refined in the fire, may result in praise, glory, and honor when Jesus Christ is revealed" (1 Peter 1:7). He also says that through suffering, we can be "weaned" from sinning (1 Peter 4:1). Trusting our lives to our faithful God during suffering can have a purifying effect on our character.

In suffering, we witness firsthand the Presence of God. In the book of Job, God doesn't answer Job's questions of "why" with a spoken answer. Instead, he responds with His very Presence. God "shows up" in the midst of suffering (Job 38-41). In the same way, Peter knows firsthand that it is God who suffers with us. For Peter, God is not aloof or distant. God is "with us" in all of our sufferings and suffers with us. Jesus, as God in the flesh, experienced suffering, and, in particular, he experienced unjust suffering. Peter says that Jesus was "rejected by men," but he was chosen and precious in God's sight (1 Peter 2:4). Jesus' suffering was actually on our behalf, or as Peter says, it was "for us" (1 Peter 2:21), the "righteous for the unrighteous," to bring us to God (1 Peter 3:18). Peter says that "Christ suffered in his body" (1 Peter 4:1), and Peter himself was a witness to the sufferings of Christ (1 Peter 5:1). Understanding God as a suffering God helps us realize that God is with us when we suffer. Peter is fond of Psalm 34, quoting directly from it that "The eyes of the LORD are on the righteous and his ears are attentive to their cry." (1 Peter 3:12). Psalm 34:18 says that "The Lord is close to the broken-hearted and saves those who are crushed in spirit." This God can be close to the broken-hearted because He knows exactly what they are going through.

In our suffering, we can "participate" with Jesus' suffering. Peter urges us to "participate in the sufferings of Christ" (1 Peter 4:13) and to rejoice when we suffer because suffering allows us to suffer with Jesus. It is at such times that "the Spirit of glory and of God rests" on us (1 Peter 4:14).

When Peter says that we should "participate" in the sufferings of Christ, what does he mean? To the churches who were first reading his letter, the suffering was a participation in Christ's suffering because they were being persecuted for being Christians. They were actually suffering on account of Jesus and, in that sense, participated with Jesus in suffering. Although Christian persecution is prevalent throughout the world today, most of the unjust suffering we experience in Western culture is not persecution. Most of our unjust suffering comes from health problems, financial issues, or the loss of a loved one. But even that sort of unjust suffering can be seen as a "participation in the sufferings of Christ" if we view suffering as an opportunity for God to use us through our suffering. We can decide how we cope with suffering. We can complain about the unfairness of it and the pain involved, or we can turn it over to Jesus and see it as a means to "participate" with Jesus' suffering. In other words, God can "redeem" all suffering and use it for good things, just like he did with Jesus' suffering. If we view our suffering in this way, the very Spirit of Jesus can "make contact" with our spirits, and we can feel the presence of God and allow Him to provide meaning to our suffering.

Our suffering can change other people. One of the ways that we can "participate" in Jesus' suffering is to see how God can use our suffering to change other people's lives. This is a critical way in which God "redeems" our suffering. Because I have gone through a particular experience of grief or loss, I can empathize with others who are going through that same grief or loss, and I can help them. My suffering has meaning and purpose. Although the final "redemption" of our suffering will only come when we see our loved ones again, when we let God use our pain, He can "redeem" it in our lives. Peter says that our suffering can significantly influence other people's lives: "Live such good lives among the pagans that, though they accuse you of doing wrong, they may see your good deeds and glorify God on the day he visits us" (1 Peter 2:12); "For it is God's will that by doing good you should silence the ignorant talk of foolish men" (1 Peter 2:15).

God Himself is our model of unjust suffering. The classic example of one who suffered unjustly on behalf of others is Jesus. It was his suffering that made us realize that God is not aloof to our suffering—God took it upon himself to experience our pain. It was Jesus' suffering that made us realize that God loves us so much he would go to the extreme measure of the cross to forgive us and woo us to him. It was Jesus' suffering that made us realize there is no sin or action that we have committed that is beyond God's ability to forgive. It was Jesus' suffering that has "redeemed" the whole world, one individual at a time. God knew that our freedom to choose would bring with it pain and suffering. Yet, even before the creation of the world, God not only provided a way for our forgiveness in the cross but also decided to "take the lead" in suffering and serve as a model of how we should suffer (1 Peter 1:20). Peter says that "Christ suffered for you, leaving you an example that you should follow in his footstep." (1 Peter 2:21). What is the example he left? *That he didn't retaliate against unjust suffering; instead, he "entrusted" himself to his Father God.* Like Jesus, we should commit ourselves to our "faithful" Creator and continue to do good (1 Peter 4:19). Jesus stands as the prime example of what God will do when someone entrusts himself into the care of God. God will "raise him up" and use his suffering to bring about blessings and good things in other people's lives.

Finally, suffering is temporary. Please don't misunderstand all this talk about "redemptive suffering." There are great things that come out of our suffering if we turn it over to God. But unless there was a "faithful" Creator who will make things right in the end, all talk of suffering is pointless and morbid. But this is what makes Christianity and the message of Jesus utterly different from any other view of life or suffering. Our hope is based not only on the death of Jesus but also on the resurrection of Jesus from the dead. The term "resurrection" or "raised" is paramount in Peter's thinking, appearing more than five times in 1 Peter. Even more than that, nine times Peter makes statements to the effect that Jesus' glory or vindication will be "revealed" or that there will be a coming day when Jesus is revealed or "visits us," when we will receive our final salvation. Peter wants us to know at the very beginning that our hope is a "living" one through the resurrection of Jesus Christ from the dead (1 Peter 1:3). It is in this hope that we greatly rejoice, though for "a little while" we may have to suffer grief in all kinds of trials (1 Peter 1:3—6). Peter says suffering is only "for a little while." Peter reminds us that we are only "strangers" here, temporary residents who will not be here forever (1 Peter 1:1, 17; 2:11).

And now for the final question.

3. How do we live?

In a word, *gloriously!* But when Peter talks about glory, he isn't talking about some emotional state that changes with the circumstances. The glory Peter is talking about is like a warm fire that glows more steadily as time goes by, a life that becomes more confident in supernatural realities as each year passes. A glory reflected in character that becomes more firm and love that becomes more unconditional.

For our everyday living, Peter uses "everyday" words as metaphors to show us how to live. This is how we are to live:

- *Like children.* We should live like children who know that they can trust completely in the heart of their Father God. We are "born again," living our journey here with new hope in this life and for life forever. Like children, we feed on the satisfying love and Presence of our God.

- *Like resident aliens.* Aliens know that they will soon return home. This world is not our home, and so we keep reminding ourselves that all of this life is temporary. We also realize that we will live forever. When you believe that you will live forever, you stop sweating the small stuff and start seeing people, jobs, and life with an eternal perspective. Jesus' words begin to make sense: "What does it profit you if you were to have everything in the world, and yet lose your soul?" (Matthew 6:26).

- *Like hopeful people.* We do not live as people without hope, but as people who know we will live forever and know that God is for us and will never forsake us. A constant theme running throughout 1 Peter is hope. As Christians, we have hope not only that we will live forever with God, but that God is "with us" in every situation in our lives on this earth. He is working to "redeem" even the worst on this earth into something good that will be "glorious."

- *Like holy people.* We are "different," we are holy. We have been made perfectly whole and clean by Jesus' sacrifice for us. Jesus' Spirit is now slowly changing our hearts so that we are whole, through and through. Another constant theme running through 1 Peter is holiness. God has made us holy and is changing our character to be like his holy character, and it is our changed character that can, in turn, change and preserve our society and culture.

- *Like chosen people.* As holy people, we are also chosen to be the "special forces" of God among the people of this world. God is training us in how to live quality, enduring, productive lives. As we grow deeper in Christ, and as our character is transformed, we permeate the world and change it.

- *Like sheep.* Like sheep? Yes, like sheep. This is encouraging to me because sheep are some of the dumbest creatures on earth. Not only are they stupid, but they stink, they're defenseless, and they're stubborn. Their only hope is to have a good shepherd who will take care of them in every way. Peter reminds us that we have a "Great" Shepherd, who is always overseeing our souls (1 Peter 5:4). When Peter wrote this, he probably had in mind the words of Jesus from John 10, who said that He calls each of his sheep "by name." Peter might also have been remembering that great Psalm, Psalm 23, where God is described as a shepherd who restores and refreshes our souls, and as a God who fights for us, rescuing us from all the threats and evil of this world. The Great Shepherd teaches us daily how to live in a wicked world.

- *Like living stones.* That may seem odd at first, but Peter is telling us that we must live together, in community, with our brothers and sisters in Christ, built up as a new temple in which God's own Personal Presence dwells.

- *Like priests.* Priests represent men for God, and so we serve one another out of love. Priests also represent God to men, so we serve the community in which we live, presenting Jesus Christ to the world.

- *Like free people.* We are no longer slaves to those passions that once ruled our bodies, hearts, and minds. Now we live confidently, without fear, free to serve.

- *Like servants.* Our model is Jesus, the Great Servant Leader who changed the world forever. In our families, our church, and our community, our first inclination is to serve others and build them up. When we have that kind of servant's heart, then we are becoming like God.

Who is Peter writing to, and what does he want to say?

Peter says that he is writing to the "exiles" scattered about in regions that today cover most of modern-day Turkey. He mentions in 1:1 five different Roman provinces: Pontus, Galatia, Cappadocia, Asia, and Bithynia. The way these provinces are listed might reveal the route that the person carrying the letter (possibly Paul's good friend Silas) would travel to deliver the letter so that all the churches could read it. Scholars have pointed out the vast geographical area these provinces cover and the widely different cultures in these areas. Citizens in these areas "had different origins, ethnic roots, languages, customs, religions, and political histories."[1] But "as diverse as the backgrounds of these people were, they had become the new people of God, the brotherhood, the chosen people scattered in the world."[2]

---

[1] J. H. Elliot, *A Home for the Homeless: A Sociological Exegesis of 1 Peter, Its Situation and Strategy* (New York: Fortress Press, 1981), 61.

[2] Edmund Clowney, *The Message of 1 Peter: The Way of the Cross* (Downers Grove, Ill: Intervarsity Press, 1988), 17.

Whether the Christians in these churches were predominantly Jewish or Gentile has been the subject of much debate. Some of Peter's statements would indicate that he is writing to Gentiles. Peter says that his readers were redeemed from "an empty way of life" handed down from their forefathers (1:18); he says that while once they were not a people, now they are the people of God (2: 10); and he says that they have spent enough time doing what pagans do, living in debauchery, lust, and drunkenness (4:3). These statements would seem to indicate the readers are Gentiles. However, some scholars have noted the extensive Jewish references that Peter makes in the letter and have concluded his readers were predominantly Jewish. Ben Witherington notes that "all the earliest commentators on 1 Peter, including the Greek Fathers in general, concluded that 1 Peter was written to an audience largely, if not entirely, made up of Jewish Christians."[3] Also, we do know that there were many Jews from these provinces who were in Jerusalem at Pentecost in Acts 2 (see Acts 2:9). The best guess is that these churches, like most of the early first century churches, were a mixture of Jews and Gentiles.

Whoever these Christians were, it is clear from the letter that they were suffering. Peter wants to provide them hope and confidence during stressful times and to remind them to look to Jesus as a model for enduring suffering. We don't know exactly what type of suffering they were experiencing, but it probably was not the official Roman persecution of Christians that would come later in the century because Peter tells his readers to submit to the emperor and to honor him (3:13, 17). We don't know exactly when the letter was written, but the early church and most scholars conclude that it was some time in the early 60s, possibly 62 or 63. Given Peter's statement that the Christians should submit to and honor the emperor, it was probably written before the general persecution of Christians by Nero in 63.

However, these Christians do seem to be suffering from persecution of some type. It may be that they were starting to feel the kind of persecution

---

[3] Ben Witherington, III, *Letters and Homilies for Hellenized Christians, Volume I: A Socio-Rhetorical Commentary on 1-2 Peter* (Downers Grove, Ill.: Intervarsity Press, 2007), 27-28.

that would eventually prevail in Roman society. Early Christians were accused of all sorts of things, including atheism (because they rejected Caesar worship and the worship of Roman gods); cannibalism (because they took the Lord's Supper); and being un-patriotic (rejecting Caesar worship). Many times, Christians were expelled from local trade guilds and were unable to continue in their occupations. We get a flavor of some of what this persecution entailed: Peter mentions that the pagans think it strange that they do not plunge into the same drunken carousing that they do (4:4); his readers are suffering a "painful trial" (4:12) and they are insulted because of the name of Christ (4:14).

These early Christians might have been experiencing similar treatment that Christians face today in modern society. We, as Christians, often make people feel uncomfortable just by our lives. Although we don't say anything that would indicate we are judging them, some people begin to hate Christians just because of the purity of our lives. Christians are often depicted in the media as hicks or "fundamentalists" who lack intelligence. Christians are often accused today of being intolerant because of their Godly views. While our society prides itself on being tolerant, in general, it is not tolerant of Christianity. Peter's letter is thus an excellent guide on how to live in a society like ours where Christians are often mocked.

Encouragement for Everyday Living

God has given us the Scriptures to encourage us so that we might have hope: "Everything that was written in the past was written to teach us, so that through endurance and encouragement of the Scriptures we might have hope" (Romans 15:4). This book is designed to glean from 1 Peter encouragement for daily living and reminders of our "living hope." Passages from 1 Peter are viewed in "bite-size" doses so that you can read each day and chew on them. There will be a little Greek thrown in so that you can get the flavor of what was originally intended by Peter. Each of these daily readings is followed by a prayer so that God will bless your daily meditation. The entire book could be read over 40 days, or it could be savored for a longer period of time. The Scriptures are amazing if we will spend the time reading, meditating, and listening to what God is telling us. May your reading be blessed, and may you know more and more the living hope that is ours in Jesus Christ! To him be the glory and the power forever and ever, Amen (1 Peter 4:11).

CHOSEN PEOPLE IN A
STRANGE WORLD

Peter, an apostle of Jesus Christ,

*To God's elect, exiles scattered throughout the provinces of Pontus,
Galatia, Cappadocia, Asia, and Bithynia, (1:1)*

In typical Hebrew fashion, the writer tells us upfront who he is: Peter, an apostle of Jesus Christ. His real name was Simon, but from the first time Jesus met him, he had come to be known as "Peter," which means "Rock." Jesus had renamed him "Rocky."

Peter also tells us who he is writing to, and he uses three words to describe his recipients.

First, they are described as *"God's elect" (elektos).* This is the same word used time and again in the Old Testament to describe the Hebrew people, the "Chosen People" of God. Out of all the nations in the world, God had chosen a small tribe of people to bless the world (1 Chron. 16:13; Ps. 105.6; Deut. 4:37; Hosea 11:10). Peter adopts this description and applies it to all people everywhere, Gentiles as well as Jews, who have been chosen by God through Jesus Christ. Thus, the ancient prophecies to which Peter will allude later in the book have been fulfilled. That means *you,* reader, should consider yourself as specially chosen by God. God takes a special interest in your life and desires that you fulfill the destinies he has for you.

Second, they are *"strangers" (parepidemois)* or sojourners in this world. A more modern word might be "resident alien," one who resides in a foreign land temporarily. Peter says that Christians should always view this life as temporary and should keep their hearts at home with God. We need to realize, especially in the midst of suffering, that this life is not all there is. We need to live "with eternity in mind" and view life as a journey towards God. The thought brings to mind the Jews who had to live in exile in Babylon after the fall of Jerusalem in 586 B.C. The prophet Jeremiah encouraged such exiles to live fully in their foreign land, for God was with them even in the foreign land, and he would ensure they returned in due time to their true home (Jer. 29:4-14). It was said that when the Jews worshipped God in Babylon, they would always face toward Jerusalem, their true home. So we must always have our faces and our hearts set "on the hope to be given us when Jesus Christ is revealed" (1 Peter 1:13). We must not lose hope, for "when the Chief Shepherd appears, you will receive the crown of glory that will never fade away" (1 Peter 5:4). William Barclay mentions a famous saying of Jesus that is not found in the Bible: "The world is a bridge. The wise man will pass over it, but he will not build his house upon it."[4]

Third, they are the *"diaspora,"* those "scattered" throughout the world in various places. Peter uses the technical term "diaspora" that was used to describe the Jewish nation that had been scattered across the globe after the Babylonian exile. Like the Jewish diaspora, Christians find themselves in places all over the world, permeating each culture like leaven works its way through the bread.

The letter is originally intended for Christians living in areas of present-day Turkey, but what was "Asia Minor" during Peter's time. The provinces are listed according to the route that the letter carrier would take once he got off the ship from the Aegean Sea. Each of these places was

---

[4] William Barclay, *The Letters of James and Peter* (Philadelphia: Westminster Press, 1996), 168.

part of Roman provinces, established by the Romans around 64 B.C. Luke tells us that on the day of Pentecost, Jews from Pontus, Cappadocia, and Asia were in Jerusalem (Acts 2:9). These converts to Christianity took the new message back home with them and founded churches throughout this region. Luke also tells us that Aquila came from Pontus (Acts 18:2). These are the churches to whom Peter is writing, churches formed and sustained by God over decades since the gospel first reached them. These first readers, formed and sustained in churches through the Spirit's power and feeding on the Good News of God's love, slowly changed their culture by impacting their world one day at a time. The culture they were in is very much like ours today—hostile to Christians and the Christian message. But God is faithful, and just as He changed the first century culture so that Christianity finally dominated and transformed the ancient world, so Jesus Christ will dominate and change the world today—one day at a time.

Father God and our Lord Jesus Christ, thank you that you have chosen me and that you are concerned about all that is going on in my life today. This is a strange world, and I know that my certain destiny is to live with you forever. But Jesus said that all authority on heaven and earth had been given to Him, and I know that He always changes the world, and my life, when we trust Him. Today I trust you, Lord Jesus, in the details of my life. I am chosen by you and special, and I know you are with me today. Thank you.

THE DIVINE CONSPIRACY

² Who have been chosen according to the foreknowledge of God the Father, through the sanctifying work of the Spirit, to be obedient to Jesus Christ and sprinkled with his blood:(1:2)

Peter reinforces the thought that we have been chosen, naming each Person of the Trinity that was involved in choosing us: Father, Son, and Spirit. This is the "divine conspiracy" of God, in which he is intent on pursuing us, choosing us, rescuing us, and purifying us. As David Hubbard expressed it, "In a massive conspiracy of grace, Father, Son and Spirit have plotted together to turn our lives around."[5] Peter mentions the three parts of this "divine conspiracy": God's prognosis of our condition; the Spirit's work to sanctify or make us holy; and cleansing by, and obedience to, Jesus Christ.

First, we have been chosen according to the "foreknowledge (*prognosis*) of God the Father." The cross was not an afterthought. Even before he created the world, God had understood all that would be involved in creating us. Out of love, he gave us the freedom to reject him, and out of love, he has used every possible means to win us back to him. This is an incredible thought! God can accomplish his divine "Yes!" in your life and to make everything work together for good (Rom. 8:29). The Greek word

---

[5] David Hubbard, *The Holy Spirit in Today's World* (Waco, TX: Word, 1973), 29.

for "foreknowledge" is also interesting: *prognosis*. You might say that God's "prognosis" for humanity is excellent, that He has made way for His ultimate good purposes to win out.

Second, his divine plan includes making us "holy," just like he is. To be "holy" means primarily to be different, but different in the way that God intended us to be: whole, peaceful, joyful, loving, giving, selfless. To be holy is to possess, in *increasing* measure, all the wonderful attributes of God, our Father. Just as parents desire their children to imitate their good character traits, so the Father desires that we should imitate him: "Be holy, because I am holy" (Lev. 19:2). But this divine plan is more than a desire of God. This divine plan for us to be holy is also a *promise* of God. God promises that through the "sanctifying work of the Spirit," he will make us the kind of people that deep down we want to be (Phil. 1:6). We are not able on our own to bring about a holy character. Only God can do this, from first to last.

Although it is the work of God's Spirit that transforms us, Peter challenges us to do certain things that will allow the Spirit to work within us:

- crave the Word of God like a baby craves milk (1 Peter 2:2);

- get rid of malice, deceit, hypocrisy, jealousy, and slander (1 Peter 2:1);

- get rid of sinful desires, which "war against your soul" (1 Peter 2:11);

- taste and see that the Lord is good (1 Peter 2:3);

- love each other deeply (1 Peter 4:9);

- use the gifts that God has specifically given to you (1 Peter 4:10-11).

Through it all, it is God the Spirit who is sanctifying us. When we fall, we must not give up, but remember the promise that he will accomplish the good work in our lives which he has promised. Jesus reminded us that we did not choose him, but he chose us (John 15:16); that we cannot bear any fruit unless we remain in Him (John 15:4); and that no one can snatch us out of his hand (John 11:28). Jesus is the one who calls us from first to last and will see us through. As Aslan, the Lion told Jill in C.S. Lewis' *The Silver Chair*, "You would not have called to me unless I had been calling to you."[6]

Third, the results of the Father's persistent choosing and the Spirit's invading work results in our obedience to Jesus Christ. We must note Peter's order here. Our obedience is a result of what God has done and is doing in our lives. We also need to understand that Peter is not talking about "obedience to rules" but "obedience to Jesus Christ." Peter wants us to realize that he is calling us to a relationship, to obedience to a living, real Person, the One who is our Brother, our Friend, our Companion, our Lover, and Rescuer. It's easy to do something for the sake of one we love, especially for one who has served us as Jesus has. Peter mentions here, as he will throughout the letter, the "blood" of Jesus. Peter had seen this blood with his own eyes, gushing from Jesus' back, side, head, arms, hands, and feet. To him, and to us, it is "precious" because it guarantees that we are holy and accepted in God's sight.

Peter's reference to the blood being "sprinkled" brings to mind the three times in the Old Testament where blood was sprinkled:

1. For *ritual cleansing,* e.g., when a leper had been cleansed (Lev. 14:1-7). The sprinkling by animal blood was a sign or seal confirming that the leper was healed. The type of cleansing we need is spiritual cleansing, which is the assurance of forgiveness and the power to change. The blood of Jesus is powerful assurance that God has forgiven us. And if he would give his own Son as an offering to take our guilt, don't you think he will stick with us until he completely transforms our character so that we can be like him?

2. For *setting apart,* or consecration, e.g., when priests were set apart to represent men to God (Aaron and the priests were sprinkled with blood in Ex. 29:20-21; Lev. 8:30). Peter will call all Christians "priests," and we are called to perform the priestly functions of sacrificing ourselves for

---

[6] C. S. Lewis, *The Silver Chair* (New York: HarperTrophy, 2000), 25.

men and to God. We are consecrated to represent people before God and to represent God to people. We are the "select team," the special forces set apart to permeate the places we work and live with grace, love, and hope.

3. For *affirming the covenant and pledging obedience.* In a great scene from the Old Testament, the people of Israel, having heard the word of God from Moses, promised that they would obey all the words spoken to them by the LORD. As a token of this covenant relationship, Moses took half of the blood of the sacrifices and sprinkled it on the altar, and the other half he sprinkled on the people (Ex. 24:1-8). The Hebrew writer picks up this same thought in stressing that since we can now have the confidence to enter directly into the Presence of God through the blood of Jesus, we should draw near to God with a sincere heart in full assurance of faith, "having our hearts sprinkled to cleanse us from a guilty conscience" (Heb. 10:19-22).

Father, Son, and Spirit thank you so much that You have conspired together to turn my life around. I believe that you can take even the bad things in my life and work them out for Your glory. I praise you that you will not rest in my life until you have taken my heart and changed it to have the same love, wisdom, peace, and joy you have. In the name of Jesus, Amen.

GRACE AND PEACE

Grace and peace be yours in abundance. (1:2)

Peter's first words to these churches (and to us) are "grace and peace be yours in abundance." The Hebrews would often greet each other by saying "*Shalom*," which means "Peace." Christian writers (and particularly Paul) added the unique Christian greeting of "Grace" (Gk. *Xaris*) to their greetings, coupling the Hebrew idea of "well-being" with the Christian concept of "grace." Peter adds his own thought that such grace and peace should be ours "in abundance." We cannot settle for mediocrity when it comes to the richness of God's blessings and grace. Dallas Willard has said that it's not the sinners who use grace; it's the saints. Willard says that the greatest saints are not those who need grace *less*, but those who consume grace the *most*, "those who are saturated by grace in every dimension of their being. Grace to them is like breath." [7]

A similar thought is found in 2 Peter 3:18, where Peter prays that we "grow in the grace and knowledge of our Lord Jesus Christ." Don't settle for the mundane in your spiritual life. May God's grace and peace be yours in abundance!

---

[7] Dallas Willard, *Renovation of the Heart: Putting on the Character of Christ* (Colorado Springs, Colo: NavPress, 2002), 93-94.

Thank you, Lord Jesus, for spilling your precious blood to bring me back to you. I thank you that, like Peter, you have great plans for me and will continue to stay with me and love me and shape me to be and do things in this life so that I will experience your Glory. I thank you that you fill me with grace and peace in abundance as I trust in You. My life is secure in Jesus' name, Amen.

HOPE TO LIVE AND A LIVING HOPE

³ Praise be to the God and Father of our Lord Jesus Christ! In his great mercy, he has given us new birth into a living hope through the resurrection of Jesus Christ from the dead, 4 and into an inheritance that can never perish, spoil or fade. This inheritance is kept in heaven for you, (1:3,4)

In typical Hebrew fashion, Peter starts with a "blessing" or a benediction (a doxology). For a millennium, Jews have begun their worship with the saying "Blessed art thou, O God," and then recite 18 things that God has done for them for which he is worthy of praise. These are called the "18 Benedictions," and these are still recited in synagogues today. To the Jew, God was worthy to be praised because of specific historical things that God had done for the people of Israel. Similarly, Peter begins with a Christian "benediction," praising God for what he has now done within history in raising Jesus Christ from the dead and imparting that same new life into our hearts and souls. He is not an "unknown" God. He is a God whom we call upon as our "Father," and who has revealed his Father-like love through Jesus.

Peter says that Father-God has given us three things that time, suffering, and even death cannot take away from us. These three things, given to us out of God's "great mercy," are:

1. *New birth*. The Greek word (*anagenesis*) literally means that we have been "born again." The word implies not only that we have been given a second chance, but that life now is entirely new and different. This new life has a quality about it that is filled with richness. Imagine a life where you were never afraid of being unloved; where God, like a Father, richly cares for all your needs and feeds your soul with His Presence; where all your efforts in life will be noticed and richly rewarded; where your failings are never brought up, but day after day you become the kind of person you want to be; where death is not overwhelming because you know that you and your loved ones will live forever. These ideas are expressed in the Greek word for "quality" life, *zoe*, and it is the quality of "life" that Jesus came to bring in abundance (John 10:10). However, this is not a rebirth that can be accomplished on our own or by our willpower. It comes only by the Spirit of God in our lives as we let Him take complete control (John 1:13).

2. *Living hope*. You can live for weeks without food, you can live for days without water, but you cannot live for a minute without hope. If you have no hope in your life, you are as good as dead. What are you hoping for? Peter here describes our hope as coming from "the resurrection of Jesus Christ from the dead." If for this life only we live, what a hopeless existence that would be (1 Cor. 15:19)! But we have the assurance of life after death because of the reality that Jesus did rise from the dead. The person who wrote this letter, Peter, was crucified for testifying to this fact. Jesus is the "first fruit" of those who are raised from the dead (1 Cor. 15:20), and all who hope in Him will someday be like Him, risen indeed! Thus, the present life takes on an entirely different color. We see things through an "eternal" perspective. This perspective doesn't make us too heavenly minded for any earthly good. On the contrary, because we know what really matters and what will last forever, we are more focused on living well in this life. C.S. Lewis said it well: "Aim for heaven and you get earth thrown in; aim for earth and you get neither."[8]

---

[8] C. S. Lewis, *Mere Christianity* (New York: Collier, 1960), 118.

The description of this hope as "living" means this hope gets more certain every day. Our hope is a "living" thing that grows as we mature. When we first became a Christian, we trusted in God because the Spirit convicted us and because there were rational reasons to believe. Our mind may very well have played a key role as we thought deeply about all of the reasons to believe in God and in Jesus Christ. But as we mature, new and exciting reasons continue to spring up that reinforce our hope. We recount how God has taken care of us, maybe especially in difficult times. God has become "real" to us in an experiential sense. We have "experienced" God in our lives, and thus our hope is living and growing the more we mature. Sometimes it's even in the midst of suffering that we have the most profound experiences of the Presence of God. Paul alludes to this when he points out that our sufferings produce character, and this character produces hope, and our hope does not disappoint us, because God's love has been poured into our hearts through His Spirit (Rom. 5:5).

3. *An "inheritance" that can never perish, spoil, or fade, kept in heaven for you.* We often think of the term "inheritance" as something we get in the future, but when the Bible uses the word, it is speaking of something that is a secure possession, and even something that can be enjoyed in part immediately. For the Israelites, the "inheritance" was the Promised Land itself, the land of Canaan, a land flowing with milk and honey. They "entered into" this inheritance, and God would urge them to "take all of the land" and not to shrink back from claiming their inheritance (see Deut. 11:24-25 and Joshua 1:1-5, 11). God himself is also sometimes described as Israel's inheritance (Ps. 73:26; Deut. 10:9). Thus, Jeremiah describes God as his "portion" or the allotment that he chooses as his inheritance (Lam. 3:22). In the same way, God told Abraham that He was Abraham's "very great reward" (Gen.15:1). With these thoughts in mind, we can see how our inheritance is something real and tangible, something that we begin to enjoy now but which we will fully enjoy when we are raised from the dead like Jesus. We enjoy it now because God is our inheritance and our portion. The Spirit and Presence of God Himself is our "down-payment," guaranteeing what is to come (2 Cor. 1:22; Eph. 1:13,14).

Father God, thank you that my life is completely new and that you renew my hope in you everyday. Everyday my hope in your constant care for me grows more and more so that my hope in you lives and renews every day. That hope grows as I find my true satisfaction in relating everything in my life to you, to spending time talking with you, in turning my worries over to you, in seeking to love others like you love me. In the name of Jesus, Amen.

YOUR DESTINY IS SURE

...into an inheritance that can never perish, spoil or fade. 4 This inheritance is kept in heaven for you, 5 who through faith are shielded by God's power until the coming of the salvation that is ready to be revealed in the last time.(1:4, 5)

Peter describes our inheritance as "kept" (*teteremenen*) in heaven, which is in the perfect participle tense. The perfect participle tense means that it is a continual action. This tense emphasizes that the inheritance already exists, is now being kept safe for us, and is now ready to be revealed.

Peter uses alliteration of three words to describe how great this inheritance is. First, it is imperishable (*aphthartos*). This word literally means that it cannot be destroyed by an invading army. Despite all the warring of this world, nothing can destroy what we will receive in heaven.

Second, it is *amiantos*, which literally means "unpolluted." Even though we may fail, this inheritance cannot be touched by our sin and failings.

Finally, it is *amarantos*, which literally means "unfading" or "not able to dry up." Although life can be dry and our spiritual life on this earth can become dry, by keeping our thoughts on heaven (where Christ is, as Paul reminds us in Col. 3:1), we realize that our inheritance cannot dry out.

But how does our "inheritance," which is kept in heaven, help us down here on earth? Peter mentions suffering often in this letter, and he reminds us we can go through this life of suffering because we have a God who has suffered with us and who will make his presence known to us intimately during our times of suffering (1 Peter 4:14; 5:10). In these verses, Peter reminds us that we are being "shielded" by God's power. God "shields" us by his power until we are safe at home with him. The word for "shield" is a military term, meaning that God stands guard around us, protecting us and caring for us. Just as he did with the Israelites in the Old Testament, God is both our shield and our rear guard (Isa. 52:12). God protects us from all sides. He is able to redeem our past and even use it for good (remember Joseph, Gen. 50:20). He is with us in our present troubles, providing comfort and tenderness to our hurts (Paul calls Him the "God of all comfort" in 2 Cor. 1:3). He has already secured our future and has our inheritance ready for us. He is the One Who was, Who is, and Who is to come!

Peter says we are shielded until the coming of "salvation" which is "ready to be revealed." Peter says the salvation of God is already an accomplished fact, ready to be revealed. In the Bible, salvation is a past, present, and future event. It is a past event because we have already been saved by Jesus' forgiveness provided by the cross. Peter says God saved us even before He created us (1 Peter 1:20). It is a present event because God is always with us to rescue us and be with us during all trials. The "salvation of our souls" is something that we are receiving now (1 Peter 1:9). That means that our souls are changing, being transformed by God to be more like Him, to have more of the *zoe* "life" of God. Finally, salvation is a future event because God's ultimate good purposes will finally triumph. We will receive new bodies to be like Jesus' glorious body!

Father, I know that I will live with you forever, so today, I will live in confidence with all the great blessings you give. Fill me with overflowing joy, knowing that you have forgiven me, you are with me, and my future is secure in you. Be my rear guard and my shield. Praise your name! In the name of Jesus, Amen.

GOD'S MANY COLORED GRACE

⁶ In all this you greatly rejoice, though now for a little while you may have had to suffer grief in all kinds of trials. 7 These have come so that your faith—of greater worth than gold, which perishes even though refined by fire—may be proved genuine and may result in praise, glory and honor when Jesus Christ is revealed. (1:6,7)

Because God is such a great rescuer, we "greatly rejoice" (*yagalliasthai*). The word Peter uses to describe our joy is rare, and is not found in secular writings until the 4th century A.D. It means "joy out of this world" or "inexpressible joy." In modern language, it is "joy on steroids." Peter is fond of this word because he uses it again in 1:8 and in 4:13. It is because of God's past, present, and ultimately future salvation that we have such great joy. But Peter does not gloss over the suffering we experience in this life. We can have this great joy even during our sufferings. Peter peculiarly describes this suffering: "all kinds" or "many-colored" (*poikolois*) suffering. This is the same word Peter uses in 4:10 when he refers to the "many-colored grace of God." Hillyer notes that whatever "color" suffering appears in, God's grace will match it and prove perfectly able to shield and help.[9]

---

[9] Norman Hillyer, *1 and 2 Peter, Jude*, NIBCNT 16 (Peabody, Mass.: Hendrickson, 1992), 33.

Barclay puts it this way: "There is a grace to match every trial and there is no trial without its grace."[10]

Suffering is difficult. No one likes to suffer. So how in the world can we find joy even in the middle of pain? Peter gives us three helpful encouragements:

1. *Because we know that this suffering is only for "a little while," and we know that the end is assured.* A person can endure anything if he has something to look forward to. Jesus' resurrection, as well as his active Presence in our lives, assures us that this life is not the final answer. Throughout history, God has always triumphed in the end. And we know that he will ultimately triumph in our lives. God can turn any crucifixion into a resurrection.

2. *Because we know that suffering can "purge" us in ways we could not otherwise be purified.* Peter likens this process to the refining of gold. A heating process purifies precious metals, and because of the heat, all the imperfect metals rise to the top and are scooped out by the smelter. How does a silversmith know when a precious metal is pure of all contaminants? When he can see his reflection in the liquid metal. In the same way, our Father purifies us in such a way until He can see his good reflection in our hearts.

Peter has an interesting twist on this idea. Although he uses gold as an example of how our faith is purified in trials, he reminds us that "gold" perishes. This might be Peter's way of asking us where our real trust in life lies. Do we trust our "gold" more than we trust God? Would our trust in God still be there if we lost our jobs, our houses, our retirement savings, or any other material thing in which we put our trust? Peter reminds us that the material security blankets of this world will all perish, and then what are we left with? It is our God who made all these things, and it is He who will make sure we have all that we need (Matt. 6:33). Thus, God can use the removal of certain material things as a means to help us see what lasts

---

[10] Barclay, 177.

forever. Paul says that we can even rejoice in our sufferings, because we know that suffering produces character, and character produces hope, and hope does not disappoint us because God has poured out his Holy Spirit into our hearts (Rom. 5:5). We can trust this purging because it comes for our good at the gentle hand of our "Father."

Jerry Sittser, in his book *A Grace Disguised: How the Soul Grows through Loss*, describes how he lost his wife, daughter, and mother all in one tragic accident. He takes the reader through his life after the accident and states: "In the experience of loss, we come to the end of ourselves. But in coming to the end of ourselves, we can also come to the beginning of a vital relationship with God."[11] Sittser says that deep sorrow "often has the effect of stripping life of pretense, vanity, and waste. It forces us to ask basic questions about what is most important in life."[12] He says that finally:

> We reach the point where we begin to search for a new life, one that depends less on circumstances and more on the depth of our souls....We begin to perceive hints of the divine, and our longing grows. To our shock and bewilderment, we discover that there is a Being in the universe who, despite our brokenness and sin, loves us fiercely.[13]

3. *Because suffering unites us in a very real way to the God of Suffering, Jesus Christ.* It is especially in suffering that we become one with the One who suffered most. Peter is fond of reminding us that Jesus was the One who was "rejected" by men, who suffered (1 Peter 1:11; 2:21-24; 3:18; 4:1-2, 13; 5:1). But he was also the One who was "chosen" by God and "precious" to Him (1 Peter 2:4). It is this "rejected" and "suffering" One who will look into our eyes and say, "Well Done!" Peter says that it will be Jesus who will give us "praise, glory, and honor" (1:7). Jesus' suffering was redemptive because it was for us. In the same way, God can "redeem" all

---

[11] Jerry Sittser, *A Grief Disguised: How the Soul Grows Through Loss* (Grand Rapids, MI: Zondervan, 2004), 90.

[12] Ibid, 74.

[13] Ibid, 90.

of our sufferings to strengthen and encourage others, which is to the glory of God.

Father God and my Savior Jesus Christ, thank you. Lord Jesus, thank you for suffering just for me. You assure me that if I were the only one in the world that needed forgiveness, you would die for me. I am overwhelmed by that. Even more, help me now in my suffering as you have promised. Assure me that there will be an end to it, that it will not last forever. Assure me that through it, you can isolate those character flaws that, like dross, need to rise to the top and be purged from my heart. Assure me with your Presence, deep in my heart, where only I can see and know you. You are familiar with suffering, and you know how to handle it. I don't. So please, in a way I can't comprehend, be with me in my suffering, and let me know you more fully through it. In the name of Jesus, Amen.

JESUS GIVES INEXPRESSIBLE JOY

⁸ Though you have not seen him, you love him; and even though you do not see him now, you believe in him and are filled with an inexpressible and glorious joy, 9 for you are receiving the end result of your faith, the salvation of your souls.(1:8,9)

What Peter says next speaks directly to us, because you and I have at least one thing in common: We have never seen the risen Lord with our own eyes. Peter, on the other hand, had seen Jesus. He had been Jesus' close friend for years. Peter had witnessed Jesus being beaten, whipped, bludgeoned, crucified, and dead. But he had also seen with his own eyes the resurrected Jesus. Peter had touched the One who overcame death. He had hugged the One Who rules the universe. But Peter reminds us that you don't have to see Jesus with your own eyes to love him! Peter echoes what Jesus told them all a week after he was raised: "Blessed are those who don't see and who believe" (John 20:29).

But how can you love someone you haven't seen? "Love" (*agape*) is the right word here because He makes his love known to us in our hearts as we trust in Him more and more. It is this love that God has "poured" into our hearts by His Holy Spirit (Rom. 5:5). This love grows just as our "inexpressible joy" grows because even during this life, we are receiving the goal of our belief, the "salvation of our souls."

Peter reminds us that we are receiving (*present tense*) this salvation *now*. Glory is not something far off, which we can only enjoy in the future. We aren't "miserable souls" here on earth, giving up all the pleasurable things in life so we can get some grand prize when we die. We certainly are assured of the unimaginable glories of heaven and living forever in the presence of God, but Christianity is not about "delayed gratification." Instead, Christianity is about a living, loving relationship that grows deeper every day as God becomes more real to us. It's not that we forego the things of this world to get a prize at the end; instead, *it is that the things of this world lose their attractiveness to us as we come to realize how hollow they are and how satisfying God is.* This realization is part of the "salvation" we are beginning to receive in this life. Suffering can help here because God often rescues our souls not despite suffering, but through suffering. Our souls are, in a sense, "saved" from depending on hollow treasures that do not satisfy or last, and are "redeemed" to live rich, full lives to the "full." Jesus said that the "thief" (the devil) steals, kills, and destroys; Jesus gives us life, and life to the full (John 10:10).

God, only you can meet my "many-colored" sufferings with your "many-colored" grace. You know what I am going through because you not only walked on this earth, but you walk with me now and will be with me every step today. I give my suffering entirely over to your nail-scarred hands and feet, asking you to redeem it. As I trust you more, I am beginning to see the reality of You and the changes in my life I so desperately need. Thank you for saving me now and forever. Amen.

A COSMIC PERSPECTIVE

¹⁰ Concerning this salvation, the prophets, who spoke of the grace that was to come to you, searched intently and with the greatest care, 11 trying to find out the time and circumstances to which the Spirit of Christ in them was pointing when he predicted the sufferings of Christ and the glories that would follow. 12 It was revealed to them that they were not serving themselves but you, when they spoke of the things that have now been told you by those who have preached the gospel to you by the Holy Spirit sent from heaven. Even angels long to look into these things. (1:10-12)

Peter next puts this whole love affair of God for us in a cosmic perspective. Peter explains in more detail what he said in the second verse of his letter, that we are chosen according to the "foreknowledge" of God. The cross was not an afterthought. The cross was part of God's plan even before He created you and me. The cross was what God had intended and knew that we needed even before the "foundation of the world" (1 Peter 1:20). The cross was predicted centuries before Jesus was born in Bethlehem. The ancient prophets predicted both the sufferings of Jesus and the "glories" that would follow (see, for example, Isaiah 53, Psalms 22, and Zechariah 12:10). Some of the things Peter mentions can help us in our spiritual journey:

1.   *We should take comfort that the ancient prophets were often confused about how God was working.* They didn't understand the whole picture, but they still pressed on in faith. Peter describes them as searching "intently" to understand what God was doing. You and I often do the same thing: "Why is God allowing this?" No matter how hard we reason, no matter how hard we pray, we cannot figure out God's ways. His ways are beyond our ways (Isaiah 55:8). One reason we can't figure it out is that God's plans often take much longer than one or two lifetimes to come to fulfillment. But even though these ancients did not see the outcome of their lives or God's ultimate triumph, we, living centuries later, do. Thus, these ancients were not "serving themselves" with their faithfulness. Instead, they were serving us. They may not have seen all aspects of the outcome of their faith, but those coming after them do. In the same way, our sufferings may only make sense when we see how they serve those who come after us.

2.   *The "Spirit of Christ" was working in the Old Testament.* We sometimes forget the Holy Spirit was active during Old Testament times. But the Holy Spirit is Eternal God, and God, through His Spirit, brought about transformation then just as He does now. God's Spirit would often come upon people in the Old Testament to achieve His purposes. What is new for us is that God has freely poured out His Spirit in a fresh, immediate way to all who call upon Him in Jesus (Acts 2:21). We should also notice that the relationship between the Father, Son, and Spirit is so intimate that Peter here refers to the Spirit as the Spirit of Christ. In the same way, Paul refers to the Spirit as the "Spirit of Jesus Christ" (Phil. 2:19), the "Spirit of Christ" (Rom. 8:9), and the "Spirit of the Son" (Gal. 4:6). God the Son existed from eternity, and the Spirit of the Father is also the Spirit of the Son, the same Spirit of God. God's Spirit was at work during Old Testament times just as much as He is working today. The Spirit of Jesus was alive and active long before Jesus was born a human in Bethlehem. We should be encouraged to know nothing God does is an afterthought. He had worked out how he would rescue humanity long before he created us.

3. *The Old Testament predicted both the sufferings of the Messiah and his ultimate triumph over death and all sin.* Peter is thinking about such beautiful ancient writings as Isaiah 53 and Psalm 22. The Great Plan of God, as predicted by the prophets, was that He would deal with our sinfulness by both condemning it and taking the punishment for it, all at the same time:

"But he was pierced for our transgressions, he was crushed for our iniquities; the punishment that brought us peace was upon him, and by his wounds we are healed" (Isa. 53: 5).

"...and the Lord has laid on him the iniquity of us all..." (Isa. 53:6).

"...for the transgression of my people he was stricken" (Isa. 53:8).

"Yet it was the Lord's will to crush him and cause him to suffer, and though the Lord makes his life a guilt offering, he will see his offspring and prolong his days, and the will of the Lord will prosper in his hand" (Isa. 53:10).

"For he bore the sin of many, and made intercession for the transgressors" (Isa. 53:12).

Peter borrows directly from Isaiah 53 in 1 Peter 2:24 when he says, "by his wounds you have been healed."

Another part of the Great Plan of God was that He himself would experience our suffering with us:

"...a man of sorrows, and familiar with suffering" (Isa. 53:3).

"...because he poured out his life unto death, and was numbered with the transgressors" (Isa. 53:12).

Another part of the Great Plan of God was that physically he would overcome death and that such resurrection would be both proof and preview of God's ultimate triumph for every living human:

"After the suffering of his soul, he will see the light of life and be satisfied.... Therefore I will give him a portion among the great, and he will divide the spoils with the strong" (Isa. 53: 11, 12).

4.   *It is this Great Plan of God that sends chills down the celestial spines of God's Mighty Host of angels.* What Peter is talking about here is something that even angels can't wait to see. By mentioning angels, Peter reminds us that we need not fear because this is a plan that is certain to happen. In the same way, Moses wasn't able to go into the promised land during his life, but he was able to see it from afar and was satisfied (Deut. 32:48ff). We also do not yet have heaven in all its fullness, but we can see it from afar.

On the night before Martin Luther King, Jr. was assassinated, he gave his "I have been to the mountain top" speech. We should pray for the same assurance he had:

> We've got some difficult days ahead. But it doesn't matter with me now. Because I've been to the mountaintop. And I don't mind. Like anybody, I would like to live a long life. Longevity has its place. But I'm not concerned about that now. I just want to do God's will. And He's allowed me to go up to the mountain. And I've looked over. And I've seen the promised land. I may not get there with you. But I want you to know tonight, that we, as a people will get to the promised land. And I'm happy, tonight. I'm not worried about anything. I'm not fearing any man. Mine eyes have seen the glory of the coming of the Lord.[14]

Most incredible God, your thoughts and plans are so far ahead of me and yet so much about me. Today, strengthen me that I will never forget that You are sovereign over all and that every one of my days is written in your book. There is nothing that will occur today that you don't know about and that you haven't already worked out a plan to bring it to a better outcome. When I think of how you had planned the cross even before you created the world, I am stunned by your incredible care and love. All we can do is cry "Glory" and rest in your power and love. Thank you, thank you, thank you. In Jesus' name, Amen.

---

[14] David J. Garrow, *Bearing the Cross* (New York: Perennial Classics, 2004), 621.

PREPARE FOR ACTION

13 Therefore, prepare your minds for action; be self-controlled; set your hope fully on the grace to be given to you when Jesus Christ is revealed. (1:13)

Peter next brings this celestial plan down to earth and gets very practical with us. Peter reminds us first of what God has done and is doing for us and then turns his attention to what our response should be. Paul also does this in his letters. For example, in Romans, after richly describing God's incredible grace for 11 chapters, Paul opens his next five chapters of practical teaching with "In view of God's mercies, therefore, offer your bodies as spiritual sacrifices acceptable to God" (Rom. 12:1). In the same way, Peter offers practical encouragement so that we may grow closer to God:

1. *Prepare your minds for action.* The word Peter uses literally means "gird up your loins." In Peter's day, men wore robes, and when they needed to do work, they would pull their robes up under their groin and tie it around their waist. We use the same kind of language when we say "roll up your sleeves." What does Peter want us to prepare? Our minds! Peter wants us to think! He wants us to use our minds. Christianity is not a mindless religion. God has called us to love him with all of our minds. Peter is stressing that our thinking is critical, just as Paul had called us to be

transformed by the renewing of our minds (Romans 12:2). Peter says that it was when we were "ignorant" that we allowed our evil desires to control us (1 Peter 1:14). Paul also said that the "Gentiles" (meaning unbelievers) have futile thoughts and "are darkened in their understanding and separated from the life of God because of the ignorance that is in them due to the hardening of their hearts" (Eph. 4:17-18). As F.F. Bruce stated, "wrong lines of conduct follow from wrong ideas about God."[15]

But we need to remember that Peter is not calling us to sit and contemplate. He doesn't call us to some ivory tower to think in the abstract about theology. He wants us to think in a way that leads to action! Peter is calling for our passionate involvement in life, engaging all of our selves, mind, body, and soul. We have to prepare our minds for action! After reading God's Word and meditating in prayer on His Word and what He wants us to do, we need to trust God and live in that trust.

2.   *Be "self-controlled."* Hillyer translates this word for self-controlled, *nephontes*, as "roll up your spiritual sleeves."[16] The verb form, *nephein*, is used in 4:7 ("be clear-minded in prayer") and in 5:8 ("be on the alert for the devil"). The thought is to take life seriously and be under control. This character trait, self-control, is a "fruit" of the Spirit (Gal. 5:22). Self-control is something we all desire. We all desire to be in better shape, watch our weight, and be more organized. We all want to control ourselves more. But we must remember that self-control is a *fruit*. A farmer doesn't "manufacture" fruit; God produces the fruit. Fruit is a "by-product" of a healthy tree, and through that healthy tree, God himself produces fruit. In the same way, self-control will elude us if we think we can achieve it on our own. Self-control comes as a "by-product" when we take the focus off of ourselves and place it on serving God and serving others. We cannot "will" self-control; our will has been too weakened by our flesh and by sin for us to attain self-control by our own discipline. Ironically, "self" control comes

---

[15] F. F. Bruce, *The Epistle to the Colossians, to Philemon, and to the Ephesians* (Grand Rapids, MI: Eerdmans, 1984), 355.

[16] Hillyer, 46.

as we take the focus off of ourselves and begin serving others in love. As Jesus said, when we give ourselves away, we find that God brings us back to ourselves (Matt. 16:25).

So how do we cultivate this fruit of self-control? Just as fruit is produced when the farmer cultivates the health of his tree, so, in the same way, self-control grows in our lives as we cultivate all the areas of our life to "let the Spirit take control." In my own life, my lack of self-control often comes when I'm selfish or bored. When I'm not involved in serving others, I begin thinking of how I might selfishly please myself. The more I think about my "self," the less control I actually have over my "self." An antidote for selfishness and boredom is love. This means that for self-control to grow in my life, I must actively engage more and more in God's love, both receiving the love of God fully and giving His love to others. I must "crave pure spiritual milk," now that I have tasted that the Lord is good (1 Peter 2:2). I must love others "deeply," being hospitable to others, using the gifts God has given me to serve others (1 Peter 4: 8-10). I should try to learn from suffering, entrusting myself to my faithful Creator (1 Peter 4:12-19). I should humble myself daily before God, casting all of my anxiety to Him (1 Peter 5:6-7).

3.   *Set your hope fully on the grace to be given you when Jesus Christ is revealed.* Another way of saying this is, "Live with the end in mind." Every day, clarify where your hope really is. Is it in your job? Is it in pleasure? Is it in your looks? Is it even in your family? No, our hope is more sure. We have the greatest of all hopes, and that is that we will live forever, and our life forever will be one of great joy and glory. If that is what we will be, we must wake up every morning, reminding ourselves of the hope that awaits us.

Peter again brings this hope back to earth. Remember, this is a "living hope." Peter says that we should set our hope fully on the "grace to be given you." The word Peter uses here is in the present participle tense, emphasizing that there is a *continual* flow of grace that comes to us and carries us through the day. We remember again that hope does not disappoint us because God's love has been poured into our hearts through his

Holy Spirit (Rom. 5:5). If we are open to God's love every day, he will assure us deep within our hearts of his reality and love for us, and that will renew our hope every day.

> *Lord, today open your Word to me. I will allow you to renew my mind as I read and meditate on your Scriptures. I know your Word is living and active and is able to pierce my soul. I need piercing. I need assurances of your Presence, grace, and power. I need to breathe and feed on your Word. Thank you for making it available to me, and for illuminating it in my soul. In the name of the Word of God, Jesus Christ, Amen.*

THE PATH TO JOYFUL LIVING

¹⁴ As obedient children, do not conform to the evil desires you had when you lived in ignorance. 15 But just as he who called you is holy, so be holy in all you do; 16 for it is written: "Be holy, because I am holy." (1:14,15)

Peter gives us the path to joyful living:

1.   *The path to joyful living begins with holiness.* Holiness is a high calling, and, at times, it is difficult. But as strange as it may sound, holiness is really what we most want in life. Holiness is a combination of wholeness, righteousness, stability, purpose, and fullness. The primary meaning of the word holy is not "morally pure" or "ethically good." Instead, the primary meaning of holiness is "different" or "set apart." But the sense of this meaning is not just different from others, but different because we are devoted to someone or something. That devotion makes us unique, special and set apart from the ordinary. Holiness can also be defined as "sacred" and "attaining a higher purpose." We might say that to be "holy" means that we are part of an "elite" team. Holiness certainly includes moral purity, but it is much more vibrant. Living with holiness means we are continuously developing within ourselves all the beautiful and fulfilling attributes of God: selfless love, joy, peace, patience, kindness, goodness, gentleness, self-control. This is the life we long to have. Frederick Buechner was right

when he wrote, "I think maybe it is holiness that we long for more than we long for anything else."[17]

Peter has reminded us that we are already holy in God's eyes. We are already children of God. God has placed his stamp of approval on us and in us, and has declared us "special," "sacred," "holy." So Peter (like Paul does) urges us to "be who we are." We are princes and princesses; we have royal blood in our veins. So let's live like the royalty we are. Let's carry on the family image. Goethe said: "If you treat an individual as he is, he will stay as he is: but if you treat him as if he were what he ought to be and could be, he will become what he ought to be and could be." In the same way, Jesus saw Simon as what he could be, a "Rock," and so he nicknamed him Peter (Mark 3:16). He also sees you as what you could be by His grace and patience.

2.   *The path to holiness comes from obedience.* We must realize how important it is for our well-being to obey God. Obedience is so much more important than any religious ritual we might perform. Just as Samuel told King Saul, "To obey is better than sacrifice" (1 Samuel 15:22). At the heart of obedience is trust—we trust God with our lives so much that we will do what he says. For example, we may feel that it would be easier to lie our way out of a situation, but we trust that God will take care of us when we tell the truth and obey him. Or we may think there is no hope for our marriage, but we trust that God will, in time, restore lost feelings when we obey him and commit ourselves to our spouse in love. Every commandment of God is a decision to trust Him or to trust ourselves. And by obeying him, we learn that God is trustworthy. When we obey, we develop a deeper understanding of God's ways and purposes in this universe. Jesus said that if we loved him, we would obey his teaching (John 14:23), and "if you obey my commands, you will remain in my love" (John 15:10). The more we obey him, the more we grow in love with him. We must also remember that what we do shapes who we are. Our actions will form a sort of "mold"

---

[17] Frederick Buechner, *Secrets in the Dark: A Life of Sermons* (New York: Harper, 2006), 242.

or "shape" around our hearts and our wills. Peter says that we should not "conform" to evil desires (1:14). This word "conform" is the same word Paul uses in Romans 12:2 when he says, "Do not conform any longer to the pattern of this world." Either we will be "conformed" or "molded" by the evil desires that war against our souls, or we will "break the mold" by offering our bodies and our minds in surrender to God's Spirit.

3. *The path to obedience is adoration.* If holiness is what we desire, and obedience is the way to arrive at holiness, how can we obey? If you are like me, I find my spirit wanting to obey, but my flesh is fighting against my desire to obey. "The spirit is willing, but the flesh is weak," as Jesus told Peter (Matthew 26:41). How can we obey? Let me ask you a question: why do children obey their parents? *Children obey because they want to please their parents and because they want to be like their parents.* Children imitate their parents (whether for good or bad). Obedience comes easier for children when they are in a close, loving relationship with their parents. Obedience happens more naturally when children are in "awe" of their parents. And even when it is sometimes hard for them to obey, it is easier when there is a loving bond between the parent and child so that the child does not want to disappoint the parent that he loves. Likewise, we need to give all our hearts as children to our Father, to desire to imitate Him and to be in "awe" of Him. Be holy because God is holy.

Henri Nouwen once asked Mother Theresa for advice on how to handle the problems in life he was facing. This was her answer: Spend one hour a day adoring God and don't do anything wrong. Nouwen realized that if he did spend an hour a day adoring God, he would be less inclined to do anything wrong.[18]

---

[18] Henri J.M. Nouwen, *Here and Now: Living in the Spirit* (New York: Crossroad, 1994), 102.

Father, what I really want is to be one with You, to realize how sacred, special, and important my life is to You. I also know I desire to be made whole in every way, to be more holy in every way. Let me spend time adoring You, reflecting on who You are and what You have done, so that You can accomplish in me that obedience I so long for. And as I obey, I will come to a deeper level of trust and love for You. Thank you. Amen.

THE FATHER'S FOREIGNERS

¹⁷ Since you call on a Father who judges each person's work impartially, live out your time as foreigners here in reverent fear.(1:17)

Peter continues the thought of our relationship as children of God, saying that we can call on God as "Father." Jesus' favorite word for God was Father, and he taught us to call on God as "Abba" (see Mark 14:35). "Abba" is the Aramaic term of personal affection for a father, much like our "Daddy." Calling God by such a personal and intimate name was extremely rare in Judaism before Jesus, and so Jesus introduced a complete new intimacy with God. The word Father implies not only affection but also that God will care for us. As Peter will say, "cast all your anxieties on him, for he cares for you" (1 Peter 5:7). Because God loves us like a Daddy, we can trust that obedience to Him is always in our ultimate best interest.

Peter says one characteristic of this Father is that he is impartial. What does this mean? We should take this in the way described in other passages of Scripture: God is fair and doesn't "discriminate" on the basis of race, status, or wealth (Galatians 2:6). God judges each person's heart by the amount of knowledge that person possesses (Rom. 2:10-11), and eventually, God will judge each person's "secrets through Jesus Christ" (Rom. 2:16). Peter learned this first hand when God summoned him to preach the good news about Jesus to God-fearing Gentiles in Acts 10. As a good Jew,

Peter had always thought that salvation only belonged to the Jews. But as the Holy Spirit fell on the Gentile believers as Peter was preaching about Jesus to them, he realized that God is the God of all nations and all peoples.

Peter says that God judges each person's work impartially. God will judge what we do here on earth. However, there are some things we must remember in considering God's judgment. First and foremost, we have already been judged and found guilty! None of us can stand in the judgment of God. We have all done things about which we are ashamed. But to our astonishment, God has declared us innocent because He Himself has already paid the penalty! We have already been judged, and the Judge is the one who pronounces us, "Not Guilty!" To our astonishment, we find that this Judge is our "Father."

Nevertheless, each person will have to give an account of his life and what we have done in this life (see Rom. 2:5-16; Heb. 4:13, 9:27). Jesus spoke of a judgment when the Son of Man would stand to judge us (Matthew 25:31-46). And on what basis will we be judged? How we have loved others! In the parable of the sheep and the goats in Matthew 25, Jesus judges us by how we treat others, and especially how we treat the "least ones," those that are hungry, thirsty, strangers, poor, sick, or in prison. The same idea is in mind here in 1 Peter 1:17. In this verse, Peter says that God will judge us according to each man's "work" (singular). As Hillyer puts it, God will judge each believer according to the scope and character of the life lived, whether it was inspired by faith or by selfishness.[19] Judgment day will reveal the kind of lives we have chosen. As Paul Johnson writes: "The last judgment is not so much delivering of verdicts as confirming verdicts already reached in the heart of each individual."[20] The apostle Paul put it this way in 1 Corinthians 4:5: "Judge nothing before the appointed time; wait till the Lord comes. He will bring to light what is hidden in darkness and will expose the motives of men's hearts. At that time, each will receive his praise from God."

---

[19] Hillyer, 48.

[20] Paul Johnson, *The Quest for God* (New York: Harper Perennial, 1996), 153.

Father, it is great to be able to call you "Father," even "Daddy." Thank you for your love for me, just like a good parent loves their little ones. Thank you also for your daily protection and care for me. Today, help me to cast all my anxieties on you, for you care for me. Please also remind me throughout the day that my life makes a difference. How I treat others is what you are concerned about, and may I feel the burden of concern for others. Remind me that how I treat the "least" person today is how I am actually treating you. Fill me with your Spirit as I rely on you throughout the day. In the name of Jesus, Amen.

NO MORE EMPTY LIFE!

¹⁸ For you know that it was not with perishable things such as silver or gold that you were redeemed from the empty way of life handed down to you from your ancestors, 19 but with the precious blood of Christ, a lamb without blemish or defect. 20 He was chosen before the creation of the world, but was revealed in these last times for your sake. 21 Through him you believe in God, who raised him from the dead and glorified him, and so your faith and hope are in God. (1:18-21)

Peter's next statements explain more clearly how we can live our lives in better expectation of this "judgment of love." The question before each of us is: where is our "treasure?" Do we find "glory" in our possessions or in serving other people? Is our hope set on perishable things, such as houses, cars, vacations, jobs, or retirement plans? Or is our hope set on every word that comes from the mouth of God, which endures forever (Deut 8:3; Matt. 4:4)? Peter describes the kind of life the world offers to us as "empty" or "hollow," and says this empty way of life has been handed down to us by our forefathers. Peter is specifically referring to the pagan life of the Gentile culture in which his readers lived. This cultural system was marked by greed, materialism, sexual promiscuity, lack of concern for life, and self-ishness. Sounds like modern times, doesn't it? Modern paganism has the same empty, hollow feel. Our culture is all about "Me" and the pursuit and manipulation of things and people to serve our own selfish needs. Such selfishness only leaves us empty and hollow, like the character in Edwin Arlington Robinson's poem, *Richard Cory*:

Richard Cory
by Edwin Arlington Robinson

Whenever Richard Cory went down town,
We people on the pavement looked at him:
He was a gentleman from sole to crown,
Clean favored, and imperially slim.

And he was always quietly arrayed,
And he was always human when he talked;
But still he fluttered pulses when he said,
"Good-morning," and he glittered when he walked.

And he was rich--yes, richer than a king--
And admirably schooled in every grace:
In fine, we thought he was everything
To make us wish that we were in his place.

So on we worked, and waited for the light,
And went without the meat, and cursed the bread;
And Richard Cory, one calm summer night,
Went home and put a bullet through his head.

We need something to shake us out of this vain selfishness. Peter says there is something that can take us out of this empty way of life, something far more precious than silver, gold, money, or possessions of any kind. To describe it, Peter uses a fantastic word with a rich meaning. Peter says that we have been "redeemed" from this empty way of life. The word "redeemed" is a commercial word and refers to the ransom price paid to purchase a slave's freedom. The word is an echo of the concept found in the Old Testament, where a Hebrew slave could be redeemed by a "next of kin" to that slave. The relative was known as a "*go el*," or a "kinsman-redeemer." In Isaiah, God is described as the kinsman-redeemer: " 'Do not be afraid…I myself will help you,' declares the LORD, 'your Redeemer, the Holy One of Israel.'" (Isaiah 41:14; see also Isaiah 43:14; 47:4; 48:17; 49:7; 54:5). The One who has rescued us from an empty way of life is Jesus. He is our "kinsman-redeemer," the One who purchases us from a hollow and empty life and provides us with inexpressible joy and a living hope.

Although we have been redeemed, Peter doesn't specify to whom this redemption price is paid. That would stretch the analogy too far. But he does say what we are *redeemed from*. We are redeemed from:

- the "empty way of life" of our past and our culture

- a meaningless life

- a culture of excess and materialism

- addictive behaviors

- guilt over our sinful past

- our fear of death.

Peter also says what we are *redeemed by*. So what was the cost of all this? What was the redemption price? "The precious blood of Christ" (vs. 19), the ultimate sacrifice of the God of all creation. The power of His love could not be contained as he burst heaven and came down. All of the punishment our sins deserved He took upon himself, and the evidence of His love is the "precious" blood of His own Son. God considers every life as precious, and so he has undertaken the ultimate sacrifice for each one of us.

Peter makes another rich association here when he calls this precious blood that of a "Lamb without blemish or defect." Peter is alluding to the Jewish feast of Passover, which began the night that the people of Israel were "redeemed" from slavery in Egypt (Exod. 12). God told the people of Israel to spread the blood of a spotless lamb over their doorposts. As the death angel passed over their houses, households with the blood on their doorposts were protected from death. In the morning, the Hebrew slaves realized that they were not only "redeemed" *from death*; they were also redeemed *from slavery*. The One who had set them free from death had also rescued them from slavery to the Egyptians! In the same way, our liberation is not only the freedom from fear of death but the freedom from any fear in life.

Peter also reminds us that God had already provided for our salvation *even before* He created us. God knew exactly how he was going to deal with our sins even before He created the world. This same thought, that God had the cross in mind even before He created the world, is repeated by Paul in Ephesians: "For he chose us in him before the creation of the world to be holy and blameless in his sight. In love, he predestined us to be adopted as his sons through Jesus Christ, in accordance with his pleasure and will" (Eph. 1:4, 5). That gives me incredible confidence in God's love.

For Peter's pagan, Gentile readers, as well as for us, God has now revealed His heart and His true nature. We don't believe in an "abstract" God that is far off and distant. We believe in a God who has shown his face. It is through Jesus that Peter says we have come to believe in God. In Jesus, we have a God who is "with us" in all our pain and suffering. He has gone to the worst corner of our lives and taken upon himself all our secrets. By his relentless love, he has broken the bonds of our guilt, our addictions, our fears, and our selfishness. The proof of this liberation is his resurrection. Peter so aptly states that it is because of Jesus that "our faith and our hope are in God."

Father, thank you that I have come to believe in You because of Jesus. Jesus reveals perfectly what kind of God You are, so loving, giving, and purposeful. Even before You created the earth and the heavens, You knew how you would save me and the entire world. You already had the cross in mind. With that kind of love, I do not need to fear today. With that kind of love, I know you can conquer my fears, habits, guilt, and sin. You are my stronghold and my refuge, my Redeemer, my savior. Thank you. In the power of Jesus, amen.

STRETCH IN LOVE

²² Now that you have purified yourselves by obeying the truth so that you have sincere love for each other, love one another deeply, from the heart. (1:22)

Peter again urges us to translate what God has done into practical, holy living. He says that we have actually "purified ourselves" by obeying the truth.

Wait a minute! I thought it was because we couldn't purify ourselves that we needed God's forgiveness in Christ? Don't we depend entirely on God's grace to make us "holy" in his sight? Absolutely! We are "saints" or "holy ones," not because of our own good deeds or obedience, but solely because of God's mercy given to us freely in Jesus Christ (Eph. 2:8). Peter himself underscores this thought when he says that Jesus bore our sins and by his wounds, we have been healed (1 Peter 2:24).

So how do we reconcile our absolute dependence on grace with Peter's statement that we have "purified" ourselves by obeying the truth? We should view this as an acknowledgment that obedience is necessary to form the character in our hearts that God so much desires. Although God loves us as we are, he does not desire for us to stay the way we are (and we should not either). The writer of Hebrews puts it well in saying that God has forever made holy "those who He is making holy" (Hebrews 10:14). John also expresses this truth when he says that it is only those who obey who love God (John 14:24). This is so because the more we grow in obedience to Him, the deeper our love for Him and His ways grow. Frederick Bruner put it this way: "Every struggle for purity through obedience to Jesus' commands is an investment in a clearer knowledge of God through Christ."[21] As Jesus said, "Blessed are the pure in heart, for they shall see God" (Matt. 5:8).

When we obey, we trust God deeper; our love for Him grows greater; our love for others also grows greater. Indeed, God is not so much after our actions as he is our hearts. It is also true that we can do the right things for all the wrong reasons. But on the other hand, our actions have a way of shaping our hearts and forming our character. The words that Peter chooses here confirm this. He says that "now that you have purified your 'souls' (*psyche*)." The word *psyche* indicates our "inward nature." As we obey God, the "truth" of how God designed the universe aligns with our very souls, and that truth is confirmed and engraved deeply upon our souls. Obedience "aligns" us with the Truth embedded in God's creation and calms our restless souls.

But we must not forget the point of all of our obedience: to learn to love as God loves. Jesus aligned the second great commandment, to love our neighbor as ourselves, with the first great commandment, to love God (Matt. 22:37). Paul says that the whole law is summed up in the command to love our neighbor (Rom. 13:9-10). We would be much more "holy" and "pure" if we remembered that all of our actions (even our "secret" ones) affect others. Peter picks up this thought by saying that by obeying the truth, we will have sincere love for others (1 Peter 2:22).

Let's try some examples of our "sins" and how they grow out of our lack of love. Sexual immorality is complete selfishness and lack of love for others. If I am sexually immoral, it is because I have cared more about myself than about my spouse, or about my future spouse. Even if I never marry, if I am sexually immoral, I am treating another person as an object instead of as a person. I have separated love and commitment from the

---

[21] Frederick Dale Bruner, *Matthew, Volume I: The Churchbook* (Dallas: Word, 1987), 148.

physicality of sexuality, something that God never intended and something that only leaves me hollow and lonely, longing for true love.

Another example is lying. If I tell a lie, I am completely ignoring the impact my lie will have on others, and I am just trying to save my skin (and not trusting in God). Think about it: if we all loved better, the world wouldn't have lawsuits, or divorces, or wars. It all boils down to love.

So how do I grow to be more loving? Peter suggests an "incubator" of love, a place where we can grow to become more loving and where our capacity for love and unselfishness can grow. This incubator is the church. Peter says that we have "sincere" love for one another and that we should love one another "deeply" (*ektenous*). The word for deeply comes from the root word that means "to stretch out," meaning that we need to get out of our comfort zone and go deeper in our love. But we are not without the best of help in growing in our love. God himself gives us the strength to love as we should.

Father, thank you for purifying my soul. My soul needs refreshment and purity, and it is by Your love that I can know I am wholly purified. I am fresh and clean in your sight, renewed to begin today fully confident in Your love. Because of that, help me to love like You have loved me. Stretch me today to love others. I know that when I do stretch to love others, I am the one that ends up being blessed. In the name of Jesus, Amen.

FEED YOUR SOUL ON GOOD STUFF

23 For you have been born again, not of perishable seed, but of imperishable, through the living and enduring word of God. 24 For,

"All people are like grass,
and all their glory is like the flowers of the field;
the grass withers and the flowers fall, 25 but the word of the Lord
endures forever."

And this is the word that was preached to you. Therefore, rid yourselves of all malice and all deceit, hypocrisy, envy, and slander of every kind. (1:23-2:1))

Peter likens our growth in loving God to the growth of a plant that needs nourishment. Before we had known the message of God's great love for us and of his power to give us a living hope, our lives were marked by selfishness and meaninglessness. All of the things that we "gloried" in ended up hollow and fleeting, here today but gone tomorrow. In contrast to such a life, we now have the very Spirit of God and His Word growing deeper in our souls. After spending too much time in fear, selfishness, and desperation, we have now been born again. As a result, the truth of the Word to which we cling becomes more certain every day. What is the "Word" to which Peter is referring? It is the "Word" that was preached to these readers. And what was that message? That God has visited us, that He is with us even in our sufferings, that He has completely forgiven us and loves us like a Father, and that he has overcome death itself. We have a "living hope," and now we cling to this "living" Word.

A beautiful flower bed cannot grow if weeds choke it. In the same way, our spiritual growth requires constant gardening. There is no other way to put it: we must be diligent in preventing spiritual weeds from choking our growth. In our spiritual journey, we not only need to "put on" those things that help us grow, such as prayer, Bible reading, time spent with other Christians, and service. We also need to "put off" those things that would ultimately destroy our lives. These may include what we watch on TV, on the internet, or in movies; influences by non-believers; gossip; jealousy; bitterness; and other things that choke our growth. Peter here uses a three-fold appeal to get rid of "all" signs of certain specific sins. He says that we should rid ourselves of *all* malice, *all* deceit, hypocrisy, envy, and *all* slander. Peter is trying to get us to see that we cannot allow any portion of that old way of life to creep back in. As Paul would put it when he spoke of anger, we cannot give the devil a "foothold" (Eph. 4:27). Similarly, Moses had warned the Israelites to remove everything that would cause destruction (Deut. 7:26).

So what are the things that Peter wants us to get rid of? He mentions five things, and each one is a threat to our *relationships*. Each one can destroy the "sincere love" that Peter urges us to have for one another. The first word, malice (*kakia*), means "hatred." You would think that we, as Christians, wouldn't be tempted to hate, and we probably don't feel any "hate" toward another. However, by our actions, we might act as if we did. To drive his point home, Peter mentions some specific ways in which our hatred may seep through. He first mentions the word "deceit" or not being truthful. In our culture, deception is prevalent. In our churches, this deception often creeps in through gossip. Peter says we should get rid of all "slander," which literally means "talk someone down." Why do we gossip? It is often a means to show that we know a piece of information that someone else doesn't know, and we want to tell it no matter what the cost to the person about whom we are gossiping. As Proverbs 18:8 and 26:22 state, it is like a choice morsel we just have to eat. However, even though we don't actually "hate" the person we are gossiping about, the crushing blow is the same to them as if we did hate them. A foul stench arises out of such "*kakia*," and Peter says to get rid of "all" of it.

Peter next mentions hypocrisy, which means that we say one thing but live another way. We seldom realize the danger that our secret sins are to our relationships. We think that our secret sins are just between God and us and that they don't affect others. But they do. Sin loves secrecy, and it grows in the dark. It is only when sin is confessed and exposed to the light that its power withers and dies. If we let our secret sins fester in the dark without admitting them to others, then that sin (whatever it is) will begin to take hold of and infect other areas of our lives. Like cancer, it cannot be compartmentalized. It eventually affects and will ultimately destroy our relationships.

Father, I desire to have a sincere, pure heart. So I pray that Your Spirit will point out to me those parts of my heart that are choking me and my relationships. Convict me and then give me the power to confess them to you and others, and then weed them out. They are killers, killing my soul, and killing my relationships. So I pray that you will weed out of me all deceit, all hypocrisy, all envy, and all slander. Fill me with Your Word and Your Spirit that I may grow up in maturity and love, just like Your Son Jesus, through Whom I pray, Amen.

TASTE THE GOODNESS OF GOD'S SPIRIT

² Like newborn babies, crave pure spiritual milk, so that by it you may grow up in your salvation, 3 now that you have tasted that the Lord is good. (2:2,3)

At the same time we "put off" our sin, we must also "put on" God's Spirit. Peter now proceeds to tell us how to "plug in" to the Spirit and let God's resources dominate our lives. How do we do this? We act like newborn babies, craving (*epipthein*) milk to grow on. The same word for "craving" is used by the Psalmist when he says that as a deer yearns ("pants") for water, so his soul craves God (Psalm 42:1). There is a hole in my soul that yearns to be filled, and only God can fill it with enjoyable nourishment. Peter uses the word "milk" to reinforce the metaphor of a baby craving nourishment. In the early church, whenever a person was newly baptized, he was clothed in white robes and was sometimes given milk as if he were a little child. Although both Paul and the Hebrew writer encourage us to move on from milk to solid food (1 Cor. 3:2; Heb. 6:2), Peter is not here trying to contrast "milk" with "meat." He is instead showing how we must crave God's nourishment and how, like a baby, we need constant feedings from God, our Father. And what is it specifically that will give us this constant nourishment? *Spiritual milk.* The word used here is the Greek word *logikos*, which means "spiritual" or "rational." Peter is saying that we should crave "spiritual milk," and most translators see this as a reference to the Word of God.

Peter says that by feeding on the Word, we will "grow up" in our salvation. What does he mean by "grow up?" Aren't I fully saved when I become a Christian? Yes, we are fully saved, but God doesn't want to leave us where He found us. He wants our souls to grow to all that He intended them to be. "Spiritual growth in salvation goes on forever, in this world and the next, for there can be no limit to the development of the soul in the fullness of what God intends by 'salvation.'"[22]

Peter urges his readers to crave God's Word "now that you have 'tasted' that the Lord is good." These words come straight from Psalm 34, one of Peter's favorite Psalms: "Taste and see that the Lord is good" (Psalm 34: 8). Peter is also using a play on words here because the word for "good" is the Greek word *chrestos*, which is a play on the Greek word for Messiah, *Christos*. There is another play on words here as well: the word *chrestos* is also sometimes used for wholesome, nourishing food (see its use in Luke 5:39). So, believers should crave the nourishing, wholesome, untainted Word of God, for it is good and healthy to the soul.

Father, today I will feed on your Word. Your Word is refreshing to my soul. It orders my soul, calms my fears, nourishes my innermost longings, and feeds my mind with pure and solid nourishment. I cannot go a day without feeding on your Word, and so I will make time to listen to what you have to say. Speak directly to me as I listen to your Word, and may it refresh and nourish my soul. In the name of the Christ, Who is my spiritual food, Amen.

---

[22] Hillyer, 57.

THE LIVING STONE

4 As you come to him, the living Stone—rejected by human beings but chosen by God and precious to him— 5 you also, like living stones, are being built into a spiritual house to be a holy priesthood, offering spiritual sacrifices acceptable to God through Jesus Christ. (2:4,5)

As Peter changes metaphors from "milk" and nourishment to "stones" and buildings, Psalm 34 is still on his mind. Psalm 34:5 reads in the Septuagint (the Greek Old Testament) as "Come to him and be radiant." Just like 1 Peter, Psalm 34 is a word of encouragement to those who are struggling, encouraging us to turn to our only real source of help. Listen to portions of this Psalm:

"The eyes of the Lord are on the righteous, and his ears are attentive to their cry....The Lord is close to the brokenhearted, and saves those who are crushed in spirit. A righteous man may have many troubles, but the Lord delivers him from them all"(Psalm 34:15, 18, 19).

Peter remembers how God has always been with those who suffer, and how those whom men might reject and persecute, God will preserve and lift up.

It is during such times of suffering that the image of God as a "Rock" is comforting. David said:

"The Lord is my Rock, my fortress and my deliverer; my God is my rock, in whom I take refuge" (Ps. 18:2)

"I call as my heart grows faint; lead me to the Rock that is higher than I. For you have been my refuge; a strong tower against the foe" (Ps. 61:2,3).

"He alone is my Rock and my salvation; he alone is my fortress, I will never be shaken" (Ps. 62:2).

Peter seizes on this imagery and asks us to "come" to Jesus, the "living" Rock, for our refuge and hope. As we do, God will also "build" us into a household of believers who can provide further strength, and together we become temples of comfort and hope for those around us.

Peter calls this "Stone," referring specifically to Jesus, as a "living" stone. How can a stone be a "living" thing? Peter is referring to the fact that Jesus is not dead but living, having overcome death. Because He is alive, we have a "living" hope. But we should also catch all of Peter's imagery here. Peter is painting the picture, as Paul did in Ephesians 3, that a "living" building is being built in this world, and this building is none other than the dwelling place of God. That temple is not a building built by hands, and it does not consist of four walls. This temple is now the church, which Paul describes as the "living organism" of Jesus' body (see, e.g., Col. 1:18 and 1 Cor. 12:12-13). This is the community of believers through whom God has changed humanity and cultures throughout the ages.

In the Old Testament, the temple was the dwelling (Hebrew *shekinah*) place of God, where His Spirit rested and from which He ruled the earth. When the temple was dedicated, God's Spirit filled the temple, and His glory and Presence was so thick that the priests were unable to enter the temple to perform their duties (1 Kings 8:10-11). The temple was arranged for the priests to offer sacrifices for their sins and the sins of the people. God was alive, and the temple was one place where his vibrant, glowing Presence was experienced. Peter has come to realize that the church is now the temple of God. No longer does God specify a particular building as the place of his Presence, but rather wherever His people (the church) are, that is where his Presence is. No longer does a priest present an offering for the sins of the people, but we have a High Priest who has gone directly into heaven on our behalf, offering Himself for our sins, once for all (Heb. 9:29). Now we all have access and confidence to enter into the direct Presence of God (Eph. 2:18, 3:12; Heb. 10:19-25). We are also all priests to serve others in response to God's love for us. We are "living" sacrifices (Rom. 12:1), offering ourselves to God on behalf of others. Now, the world experiences the Presence of God by seeing his *shekinah* glory glowing in our hearts. The impact of God's Presence is multiplied when we band together, a household, a family, a new people of God, a force that the gates of Hell cannot overcome (Matt. 16:18).

Lord Jesus you are my Rock. You are also the cornerstone on which all of civilization is built. As the steady Rock on which all of life can be built, you are also calling us all to come together. You are bringing together a new family, a new temple, a community of love where Your Spirit dwells. Impress upon me today how much I need other Christians, how much I grow when I am involved in others' lives. Forgive me for dwelling only on my own needs and call me out to open myself up to my fellow brothers and sisters in Christ. Give me a good friend today so that they can see Christ in me, and I can see Christ in them. I love you. Thank you. In Jesus' name, Amen.

JESUS IS A ROCK

⁶ For in Scripture it says:
"See, I lay a stone in Zion,
a chosen and precious cornerstone,
and the one who trusts in him will never be put to shame."

⁷ Now to you who believe, this stone is precious. But to those who do not believe,
"The stone the builders rejected has become the cornerstone,"

⁸ and, "A stone that causes people to stumble
and a rock that makes them fall."
They stumble because they disobey the message—which is also what they were destined for. (2:6-8)

Peter sets the stage by saying that this living Stone was the one who, while rejected by men, was chosen by God and precious to him. Although all seemed lost for Jesus while he hung on the cross, it was precisely through his suffering and humiliation that God "built" the church on Jesus' bloody back. "Peter had learned that the death of Christ was not an unthinkable defeat for the Son of God and the Kingdom of God. Rather, by the cross and the resurrection, God's eternal purposes of salvation had been fulfilled."[23]

Peter is bringing together two thoughts. The first is that Jesus is the "cornerstone." In Peter's day, all buildings were made of stones or bricks, and the cornerstone was the critical stone upon which all the other stones were fitted so that the building would stand firmly secure. In the same way, Jesus is the "cornerstone" upon which is built the new Temple, that is, the church, where God dwells by his Spirit. But Peter is also adding a second thought: Jesus is a "scandalous" stone, having suffered in the manner he did. Peter calls to mind Old Testament passages in which Israel was described as a "scandal" to the nations because of their suffering at the hands of the nations and at their "smallness." Isaiah had predicted that Israel, the stone that the nations rejected, would become the cornerstone (Isaiah 28:7). And God, in the end, did come to the rescue of suffering Israel.

The three Old Testament passages which Peter quotes were passages that Jesus first applied to himself, and they were very familiar to the early church. The first is Isaiah 28:16, and in this passage, Israel is the "chosen foundation stone," laid preeminently in "Zion," the hill in Jerusalem upon which the Temple was built. A very critical part of this verse is the promise that God will uphold those who trust in His power to come through: "and the one who trusts in him will never be put to shame." Peter is encouraging his readers that, despite their suffering, they will not be disappointed if they keep their trust in the Rock of Israel.

But Peter had also heard his Master quote another Old Testament scripture that contained the words "stone" or "rock." This passage was Psalm 118. Psalm 118 was a favorite Hebrew "*Hallel*" Psalm ("*Hallel*" referring to "praising God"), recited during the Passover. The thought that runs through Psalm 118 is that God would redeem Israel from its suffering, and although Israel may be rejected by the nations, it would be a rock that would cause the world to stumble because God would be her Deliverer and would build the Temple to bless the world. Thus, Psalm 118 was recited by

---

[23] Clowney, 85.

the Jews to refer to themselves, and the "rock" in Psalm 118 was the nation of Israel.

Jesus, however, had used this Psalm as a way to show the nation of Israel that he was the "cornerstone" that was rejected by men but upon which the new temple would be built (in Matthew 21:42ff, Mark 12:10ff, Luke 20:17ff). When Jesus quoted this passage, he had just told the parable of the wicked tenants. In the story, the landowner had sent his own son to the wicked tenants, but they had rejected him and killed him (Matt. 21:33-41). Jesus utilized this passage to show that it was he, and not the nation of Israel, that was the real cornerstone of God's building. He was the rock that, while rejected by Israel and the Romans, would be the foundation stone for God's work in the world. The Jews were the "builders" who rejected God's Messiah, and Jesus was the cornerstone. Peter had heard Jesus quote this just days before he went to the cross, and Peter recited it again weeks after Jesus' resurrection when he addressed the Jewish Sanhedrin (Acts 4:11).

The last Old Testament verse Peter quotes is Isaiah 8:14, the backdrop of which is Isaiah's prophecy that God would send an "Immanuel," or a "God with us." In Isaiah 8:10, Isaiah scoffs at the nation of Assyria, telling Assyria to go ahead and make their plans to destroy Israel, but it will not happen, for "God is with us." But Isaiah then immediately turns to Israel and tells them not to fear the nations around them: "The Lord Almighty is the one you are to regard as holy, he is the one you are to fear..." (Isaiah 8: 12, 13). God will be their "sanctuary," a stone that causes men to stumble and a rock that makes them fall (Isaiah 8:14). Isaiah was encouraging Israel that if they hid under (and thus trusted in) the Rock of Israel, the forces of the world would stumble over and be crushed by this Rock. Jesus also used this same passage to refer to Himself when he predicted that "everyone who falls on this stone (i.e., Jesus) will be broken to pieces, but the one on whom it falls will be crushed" (Matt. 21:44; Luke 20:18).

How are we to understand what Jesus said in the Gospels and what Peter says here? First of all, Jesus is the "Rock," our sanctuary and cornerstone. But Jesus is also a "stumbling" stone to most of the world. The fact that the Messiah would be crucified was, in the words of Paul, a "scandal"

(1 Cor. 1:23). This word, *scandalon*, is the same word Peter uses here when quoting Isaiah 8:14: "A stone that causes men to stumble *(proskomma)* and a rock that makes them fall *(skandalon)*." The word *skandalon* was also the word Jesus used when rebuking Peter when Peter tried to persuade him not to go the way of the cross: "Get behind me, Satan! You are a stumbling block *(skandalon)* to me; you do not have in mind the things of God, but the things of men." (Matt. 16:23).

We need to make two applications here. First, it is scandalous that God Himself would suffer for the humans he created, but it is only in that suffering that we have hope. We cannot climb out of our sinful situation on our own; God himself must get his "hands dirty" and suffer for us, and we are humbled by that grace. In the words of Paul, Jesus humbled himself and became obedient to death, even death on a cross! (Phil. 2:8). In the words of the writer of Hebrews, Jesus is not ashamed to call us brothers and sisters but suffered in flesh and blood just like us (Heb. 2:11). We have a God who is with us, going to our sinful corner and washing us clean by his loving suffering for us.

The second application is that God also calls us to go the way of the cross: "Whoever would follow me must take up his cross and follow me, for whoever would seek to save his life will lose it, but whoever loses his life for me will find it" (Matt. 16:25). Incidentally, Jesus made this statement right after he had rebuked Peter for trying to stand in the way of Jesus going the way of the cross. Peter could probably still hear the sound of Jesus' voice when he penned this letter of encouragement, reflecting on how Jesus had been faithful all through Peter's life.

We must also deal with this last part of this passage: "They stumble because they disobey the message, which is what they were destined for." Peter is not saying that those who disobey had no choice in the matter. The Bible nowhere speaks of a "predestination" in which God's will overcomes our free choice. Instead, "Peter's meaning is that the stumbling to disaster is the inevitable consequence of persistently refusing to obey Christ."[24]

---

[24] Hillyer, 64.

If people refuse the only possible hope that they have, the hope of God's mercy and forgiveness, what hope do they have left? "It is their choice, not some out-of-character forward-planning by God, which determines their end."[25]

Father, I am amazed today at the scandal of your love for me. How can I ever doubt you when you have loved me in such an embarrassingly unselfish way. It blows my mind to think that the God of all creation would stoop to suffer in such a scandalous way as to die on a cross for me. The depth of that suffering shows me that my sin is not too great for you to love me. The depth of that suffering shows me that you will go to whatever length to win my heart. It also shows me that you are with me no matter how much I might suffer on this earth. You know suffering. In light of that kind of love, let me trust you today. More than that, strengthen me to be like you, giving myself for others, and if need be, suffering for others. In the name of Jesus, Amen.

---

[25] Ibid.

YOU ARE GOD'S PRIESTS

⁹ But you are a chosen people, a royal priesthood, a holy nation, God's special possession, that you may declare the praises of him who called you out of darkness into his wonderful light. 10 Once you were not a people, but now you are the people of God; once you had not received mercy, but now you have received mercy. (2:9,10)

You can almost hear Peter's change of voice when he turns from describing those who refuse God's mercy, whose lives are hollow and meaningless, to describing his readers (and us). He says, "But you!" Who are we? We are a chosen people (*genos elekton*), the "elect." In the first verse of his letter, Peter called his readers "the elect," echoing Deuteronomy 14:2: "The Lord your God has chosen you to be his special property from all the nations on the face of the earth." Isaiah 43:20-21 uses this same expression: "because I provide water in the wilderness, and streams in the wasteland, to give drink to my people, my chosen, the people I formed for myself, that they may proclaim my praise." Just as the tiny nation of Israel was "chosen," now all who call on the name of the Lord, regardless of race, color or nationality, are "chosen" and precious to God. Think about it: God has chosen you. And those whom God chooses, he fights for, protects, defends, loves, cares for, and will love forever. You are chosen and precious in God's sight, so feel chosen today!

Peter also says that we are a "royal priesthood," combining both the offices of the King and the priest. The echoes here come from Exodus 19:6 and 23:22, and the phrase "royal priesthood" could also be translated as "a kingdom of priests." We should not miss the idea that we are part of the royal family, and because of our King, we have all the privileges of princes and princesses. The King fought for us and has won every victory for us.

However, as royalty, we do not sit around, letting others serve us. Instead, we are "priests," meaning that we serve others for God's sake. A priest's duties included coming before others on behalf of God, and coming before God on behalf of others. The primary purpose of the priest was to serve God and have access to Him. Peter is saying that we are now all priests. We now all have access to the Father through One Spirit (Eph. 2:18, 3:12; Heb. 10:19-25). Having that direct access, we are now all servants of one another, offering our own lives as living sacrifices (Rom. 12:1).

Peter also calls us a "holy nation, a people belonging to God." The word "holy" means "set apart," and we are set apart and belong exclusively to God. In saying that we "belong" to God, Peter uses the word "*peripoisin*," which suggests a jewelry collector who has found one prize of great value. This word brings to mind Jesus' parable of the pearl of great price (Matt. 13:44ff). We often think that this parable is referring to us as the ones finding the kingdom of God. However, the early church often saw Jesus' intention as describing how God had found us and had given all He had to purchase us. We should feel chosen and precious to God, who gave up everything in his Son for us!

Peter's words recall the beautiful passage of Isaiah 43:21, which says that we declare the praises (the *aretas*) of him who called us out of darkness into his wonderful light. The word *aretas* also refers to "victorious achievements." We declare the achievements of God: he overcame our sin, guilt, addictions, meaningless, hopelessness, and even our death! These victorious achievements have already been accomplished for us, and now he "calls" each of us to come out of our darkness and into his wonderful light. Life without God and His love is appropriately called "darkness." A life marked by hopelessness, futility, lack of love, lack of meaning, addiction, ruined relationships, and death can only be described as "dark." But we do not live anymore in the darkness—we have been called to stay in and live forever in the light! Peter's use of the word "light" indeed calls to mind the glorious "*Shekinah*" (dwelling) of the Presence of God. The light of God's *Shekinah* shone so brightly that Moses' face had to be covered whenever he came out of the Presence of God because his face was too bright for the people to look at (Ex. 34: 29-35). God is calling us to live no longer in futility, addiction, despair, and darkness, but to always reside within His glorious Presence.

Peter's use of light imagery is appropriate for Peter's other descriptions of the people of God: stones and priests. In the Old Testament, the light of the *Shekinah* is often associated with precious stones (see Ezek. 1:16, 26, 10:1; Rev. 21:18-26). Also, the priests' breastplate had precious stones covering over where the priests' heart was (Ex. 39:2-7). Thus, when the priest entered into the Presence of God, he would carry with him the precious stones. "One of the values of the precious stones in the high priest's breast piece was their ability to reflect light, and the light most readily associated in the Jewish mind in this context would be the light of the *Shekinah*, the divine Presence."[26]

Peter's last phrase (that now we have received mercy) calls to mind a beautiful passage from the Old Testament book of Hosea, the story of Hosea and his wife, Gomer. God had told Hosea to marry Gomer, who was a prostitute, to show the love God had for the people of Israel. Just as Hosea would continue to love Gomer even though she had betrayed Hosea and had run off with other lovers, so God loves us. Now, God has called beyond the borders of Israel and is calling all of humanity into his love and light. Just as Isaiah predicted, "the people in darkness have seen a great light, on those...a light has dawned." (Isa. 9:1-2; Matt. 4:15-16). Once, Gentiles were not included in the people of God. Once, we were "not a people," but now we are the people of God. And just as Gomer once was "not loved," so we did not know or experience the love of God. But all that is over. Now, all

---

[26] Hillyer, 69.

who call on the name of the Lord Jesus are "the people of God," and we are the ones who "are loved."

In sum, Peter has explained how the promises initially given to Israel are now ours. The Jerusalem temple of stone is now replaced by the living stones of the new spiritual temple of believers. The priesthood, formerly limited to the tribe of Aaron and engaged in offering animal sacrifices as the means of approaching God, is now a royal priesthood shared by all believers, who enjoy direct personal access to God. They are individually able to offer spiritual sacrifices, acceptable to God because they are made through the perfect sacrifice of Christ. God's chosen people are no longer confined to the physical descendants of Abraham...but by divine decision they are now the body of Christian believers.[27]

Father, thank you for searching for me and pursuing me, for never giving up on me, and for loving me with steadfast, intense love. Thank you for finding something beautiful in me and being patient as you work to continue to bring out the beauty in my soul. I feel loved, confident, and hopeful because I have come to know You through Jesus Christ. May I serve You today as a priest, serving others and having direct, constant access to You. In the name of Jesus, Amen.

---

[27] Hillyer, 70.

BE CAREFUL WITH YOUR SOUL

11 Dear friends, I urge you, as foreigners and exiles, to abstain from sinful desires, which war against your soul. 12 Live such good lives among the pagans that, though they accuse you of doing wrong, they may see your good deeds and glorify God on the day he visits us. (2:11,12)

Because we are chosen and precious, we are the new temple of God's Spirit. We are also priests serving others, and we are light in a dark world, Peter again gets practical. He calls us by a tender name: "Beloved" (*agapetoi*) (the NIV word "dear friends" is weak). Peter wants to urge us, or to "come along side us" (*parakalein*) and encourage us.

In telling us how to live, Peter chooses some "strange" words to describe how we should consider ourselves. He says we should live as foreigners and exiles, or strangers and aliens (*paroikous kai parepidemous*). His words echo God's call to the Israelites that the land they inherited was not theirs, but God's. They were only "tenants," and they were not to set their hearts on the land: "for you are strangers and sojourners with me" (Lev. 25:23). An early church writing from the 2nd century, the *Epistle to Diognetus*, says, "The Christians dwell in their own countries, but only as sojourners. As citizens, they share in all things with others, and yet endure all things as foreigners. Every foreign land is to them as a native country, and every land of their birth as a land of strangers."[28]

So, practically speaking, what does it mean to be an alien in the world? We are to "abstain" from "fleshly lusts" which "war against our souls." The word for "abstain" means to "keep away from." Peter is giving us practical ways in which to "rid ourselves" of our old nature. To "abstain" means to put a hedge or a margin around ourselves. The verb is in the present tense as well, meaning that we need to be always in the practice of guarding ourselves and keeping a distance between our souls and those things that would destroy us.

By using the term "fleshly lusts," Peter is saying we should not let our bodies and our flesh become an idol. By saying that the "flesh" makes war against our souls, Peter is reminding us that there is a vital connection between our bodies and our psyche. As Dallas Willard writes, the soul (psyche) is that dimension of ourselves that interrelates our mind, body, and social context.[29] Our body, mind, spirit, and soul are intricately connected. What we do with our bodies has a lasting impact on how we think and feel.

The result of letting the flesh overcome us is evident: the desires of the flesh will "war" against our souls. Peter recognizes the vital connection between our bodies and our psyche or our souls. We cannot give into sensual sins without it taking a heavy toll on our psyche. Paul also stressed how closely our body and our souls are intertwined when he said that the person who commits sexual sin sins against his own body (1 Cor. 6:18). But the Good Shepherd has come to restore our "souls" (Ps. 23:3) and to give "life" to the full (John 10:10). Paul tells us that just as we used to offer our bodies in slavery to impurity and ever-increasing destruction, so now we should offer our bodies in slavery to righteousness, which leads to holiness (Rom. 6:19). The body is God's beautiful creation, but the body is satisfied only when it is in submission and obedience to Him.

---

[28] Epistle to Diognetus; Anon., 2nd century

[29] Dallas Willard, *Living in Christ's Presence: Final Words on Heaven and the Kingdom of God* (Downers Grove, Il: Intervarsity Press, 2014), 121.

Peter also recognizes that our private conduct has a powerful impact on those around us. As St. Patrick used to say, "Preach the word, and if necessary, use words." Peter says that we should live such good (*kalos*) lives among the "pagans" that although they may make accusations against us, they will end up giving glory to God. The word *kalos* means not only good or attractive but also genuine and honest. The world is always watching us, and the world can spot a phony a mile away. But people are attracted to authentic, honest people. None of us can live perfect lives. But what is good and attractive is when we are genuine, admitting our mistakes, and admitting our need for God's grace.

The culture in which the church finds itself today is becoming more and more like the culture of the first-century. The culture surrounding the early church was hostile to the moral teaching of the church. Promiscuity, abortion, euthanasia, and homosexuality were not only acceptable behavior but were encouraged. The early church was also falsely accused of such things as cannibalism (because they ate the flesh and drank the blood of Jesus), atheism (because they didn't bow to the Roman gods), damaging trade, and treason (because they did not bow to Caesar). Christians today are also falsely accused by a hypocritical world of being intolerant and narrow-minded. Those who speak out publicly in favor of the sanctity of marriage between a man and a woman are attacked and sometimes physically threatened. In the midst of all of this, we must be careful that in all the rhetoric, the outside world does not miss the truth of God's grace and the goodness of the good news. It is often said that people do not care what you know until they know how much you care. Peter reminds us that what attracts people to the good news is the simple, quiet life that shows the enduring qualities of love, honesty, and faithfulness. Lives devoted to God will, in time, prove the truth of God's Word and His Ways. Our lives must be the platform on which our words can get through to people. That is exactly what God did when He took the form of a man and came humbly to the earth. He could have shouted His commands from heaven, but he chose to live humbly, and lovingly, among us. It was this life of Christ, lived out daily by the Christians, that slowly but surely transformed the brutal Roman society into a culture that shaped Western civilization.

Father, today, I open my heart to your Spirit to take control. I know that the things of this world are temporary, and if I try to find my satisfaction in them without you, they will begin to control me. I know that if I let my passions run loose without putting them under your control, they will war against my soul and begin to destroy it. I don't want that; I want your peace, your satisfaction, your holiness. So, I open my heart to your Spirit to take control. May my life be such that others will see you in me and may my actions bring glory to you. In Jesus' name, Amen.

HOW TO MAKE AN IMPACT

13 Submit yourselves for the Lord's sake to every human authority: whether to the emperor, as the supreme authority, 14 or to governors, who are sent by him to punish those who do wrong and to commend those who do right. 15 For it is God's will that by doing good, you should silence the ignorant talk of the foolish. 16 Live as free people, but do not use your freedom as a cover-up for evil; live as God's slaves. 17 Show proper respect to everyone, love your fellow believers, fear God, honor the emperor. (2:13-17)

Peter will now give us more practical advice on how the "good" life should be lived. Ironically, this good life comes as we "submit" ourselves. In these and the following verses, Peter urges us to "submit" in four types of relationships: as citizens (to the government); as employees (his immediate address is to the slaves of his day); as servants of God, submitting to Jesus; and as spouses (his immediate address is to wives).

The word "submit" does not sit well with most of us. In today's world, we like to be our own master, and we don't like anyone telling us what to do. But Jesus teaches us that submission and service are the keys to greatness: "Whoever wants to be great among you must be your servant, and whoever wants to be first must be slave of all" (Mark 10:43). Submission is not something that Christians should resist but is instead something that brings us closer to the character of God. Jesus is our model of submission and servanthood: "For even the Son of Man did not come to be served, but to serve, and to give his life a ransom for many" (Mark 10:45). He, as our Master, put on the robe of a slave and washed our feet and suffered for us (John 13; Phil. 2). We should note that Jesus did not serve out of weakness but from a position of strength. He "knew where he had come from and where he was going" (John 13:1), and he was "in very nature God" (Phil. 2:6). In the same way, when we submit to others, whether it is to our employer or our spouse, we are not doing it out of weakness, but as a sign of our seeking to honor God and to bring him glory.

The first relationship Peter mentions is our relationship with the government. Peter, like Paul, urges us to be good and useful citizens in the country where we live. Peter recognizes that the government is instituted to punish those who do wrong and commend those who do right. Paul also understood that every ruler was put there with God's approval and under God's control, and the government is ultimately responsible to Him (Rom. 13:6-7). As Barclay notes, "According to the New Testament, life is meant by God to be an ordered business, and the state is divinely appointed to provide and maintain that order."[30]

There has always been a tug of war between the spiritual force of God's Kingdom and the human desire to establish earthly kingdoms in his name. When Peter wrote his letter, this was a hot issue. The Jews had for years lived subject to governing rulers, and during Jesus' time, there were many "Zealots" seeking to overthrow the Roman government. Even John the Baptist wondered if the way Jesus was operating was the way of the Messiah: "Are you the one who is to come, or should we expect another?" (Luke 7:19). After Jesus' resurrection, even the apostles wondered if he was going to restore the kingdom to Israel (Acts 1:6). But Jesus had a far greater vision than just winning the land for Israel. He had a far grander plan than just earthly kingdoms and glory. His vision included the whole world and all humanity. Jesus had told Peter to put his sword up—the sword is not the way of the Kingdom (John 18:11). The way of the Kingdom is one of service, submission, and suffering. The Kingdom is not brought in by force,

---

[30] Barclay, 205.

but by God's Spirit through the suffering of the cross. The kingdoms of the world come and go, and like the flowers of the field, their glories fade and die away. But the Kingdom of God blooms in the hearts and souls of people, and that Kingdom will last forever.

So what should we do in the meantime, until the coming of the Kingdom in its fullness? We should live out the "Kingdom" among those around us. We should consider ourselves as "strangers" and "aliens" in this world. And we should submit, "for the Lord's sake," to civil authorities. By doing this, God can accomplish at least two things:

1. *Our humble attitude silences the foolish talk of evil men.* Our humble attitude serves the purposes of God. Rhetoric and talk of power do not change anyone but rather divides and creates barriers. As we are humble and serving, the hearts of those who might speak against Christians become soft and receptive to the good news of God's love, and thus the Kingdom is spread in that way.

2. *We are ultimately free, no matter who is the governor, the President, or our boss.* Peter urges us to "live as free men." The majority of Peter's original readers were probably slaves, and yet he calls them to "live as free people." How can that be? Because when we fear God, we don't fear anyone else. God is the ultimate decider of our destiny, not people. Thus, in our society, we never take vengeance into our own hands; we let God be the judge. In the same way, if people persecute us, we entrust ourselves to God. Thus, we should "fear God" but show honor and respect to everyone. In this way, people have no control over us, and we have no fear of anything.

Two critical questions strike us in applying this passage to our lives today:

1. *How does this passage apply to a democracy?* When Peter wrote this passage, the Roman government was ruled by an aristocracy, and would eventually become a dictatorship. But today, many Christians (particularly in the West) live in a democracy. What should we do today? For

the Lord's sake, we must shoulder our responsibility and participate in the government we have been given. A democracy surely is a gift of God if its citizens are responsible and participate. There should not only be subjection on our part, but there must also be participation, cooperation, and civility. As Glenn Tinder argued, "The notion that we can be related to God and not to the world--that we can practice a spirituality that is not political--is in conflict with the Christian understanding of God."[31] Christian values provide the moral foundations for our society, and so our nation cannot survive if we, as Christians, see our beliefs as merely a private matter that have no real-world impact. But our engagement in politics should be cautious. The following are guidelines for Christian involvement in, and understanding of, politics:

First: Love, not power, should be our primary goal in any political activity--the transforming love of God. Thus, Christians should always be civil in their political discussion, and Christians should be a refreshing relief of kindness, humility, and civility.

Second: Christianity teaches us that humanity is sinful, and thus we cannot trust any political party or ideology: "Christianity implies skepticism concerning political ideals and plans. For Christianity to be wedded indissolubly to any of them...is idolatrous and thus subversive of Christian faith."[32] As Christians, this requires us to be as critical of our particular political party as we are of opposing political parties. Unfortunately, politics favor winning over truth and civility, but for a Christian, God's truth and love are more important and more enduring than winning a particular election.

Third: We should allow room for God to work in history despite whatever political party is in power--we do not worry that all is lost because the opposition party is in control. Because God is sovereign, we can be hopeful for the future despite humanity's problems. Our culture puts too

---

[31] Tinder, Glenn, "Can We Be Good without God?" *Atlantic Monthly* (Dec. 1989); For an excellent discussion of these topics, see also Glenn Tinder, *The Political Meaning of Christianity: An Interpretation* (Baton Rouge: Louisiana State University Press, 1989).

[32] Id.

much emphasis on political action, as if programs can change humans and as if politics can fix everything. Christians know that the transformation of society begins with the transformation of individuals through the unconditional love of God. As Christians, we are not panicked but hopeful. We can leave room for God's judgments in history.

Finally: We must be involved in a local church. Politics is not the hope of the world; the church saved by and submitting to Jesus Christ is the hope of the world. The church is God's way of showing the world what a group of people should look like--it is the place where the grace of God has changed lives and families, and where the world can see the face of Jesus Christ. As Peter put it, we in the church are "resident aliens" who, by our transformed lives, pique the curiosity and envy of a depraved world: a place where the world can "see your good deeds and glorify God" (1 Peter 2:12). We do good things because God's love has changed us, and by doing good, we "silence the ignorant talk of foolish people" (1 Peter 2:15). Our goal is not to convince people intellectually that there is a God, but to be "prepared to give an answer to everyone who asks you to give the reason for the hope that you have. But do this with gentleness and respect, keeping a clear conscience, so that so that those who speak maliciously against your good behavior in Christ may be ashamed of their slander" (1 Peter 3:14-16).

2. *What happens if the government tries to force us to do something against God's will?* When Peter and Paul wrote their epistles, the Roman government had not yet degenerated to the point that it ultimately would. When we read Revelation, we sense much more of a resistance to the Roman government than when we read the epistles. Thus, we should remember that being urged to obey the civil government does not mean that we should do so if it means disobeying God. The Bible provides many examples in which God's people are commended for defying civil authorities (Exod. 1:17; Dan. 3:13-18; 6:10-24; Acts 4:18-20; 5:27-29; Heb. 11:23). Thankfully, in most Western cultures of today, we are not faced with this dilemma yet. As Jesus urged us, we should "render to Caesar the things of Caesar, and to God the things of God" (Matt. 22:21).

Father, today I pray for our government and all those who are in authority. I pray for wisdom for our leaders, and I pray for civility among them. I know that power has a tendency to corrupt, so I pray that our leaders will see themselves as servants and will humble themselves in your sight. I pray for a revival in our nation, with your Spirit transforming human hearts and changing our culture. I thank you for the democracy that we enjoy here in this country. Let me not take it for granted, but let me participate with love and service so that I can bring honor to your Name. In the name of Jesus, Amen.

SLAVES AND EMPLOYERS

[18] Slaves, in reverent fear of God, submit yourselves to your masters, not only to those who are good and considerate but also to those who are harsh. 19 For it is commendable if you bear up under the pain of unjust suffering because you are conscious of God. (2:18, 19)

We come now to the part of his letter in which Peter addresses most of the people who were the first readers of his letter: slaves. In Peter's time, there were as many as 60 million slaves in Roman-occupied territory. Slaves were initially the people that the Romans conquered. As the Roman empire grew, so did slavery. Slaves did all of the work in the Roman territory. A "free person" did no work at all. Slaves were not only those who did manual labor, but slaves were also doctors, lawyers, nurses, teachers, musicians, and other "professionals." The Roman attitude was: why should the conquerors do any work when a slave could do it? Slavery in the Roman empire generally was not the horrendous tragedy of slavery that it was in Europe and North America in the 18th and 19th centuries. Slaves in the Roman empire were not always treated badly. Many slaves were loved and trusted members of a household. However, the slave had no rights whatsoever. Slaves were not allowed to marry, but they could cohabitate. Children born out of such cohabitation were the "property" of the master, not the parents. A slave was not considered a person but was considered a "thing" or a piece of property. Aristotle even said, "A slave is a living tool, just as a tool is an inanimate slave."[33] Peter Chrysolgus wrote: "Whatever a master does to a slave, undeservedly, in anger, willingly, unwillingly, is judgment, justice, and law."[34] Against this backdrop of the first century's view of slaves, Peter's words in verses 16 and 17 to "live as free men" and to "show proper respect to everyone" is striking. As Jesus had taught him, Peter considered all people as having human dignity and worth. Christianity gave birth to our modern notions of individual rights and liberties through its emphasis on the dignity and worth of every human.

But one question we must wrestle with is, "Why didn't Christianity speak out strongly against slavery?" Paul encourages Philemon to free Onesimus, but he doesn't insist on it (Philemon 21). Why not? As Barclay puts it:

> To have encouraged the slaves to rise against their masters would have been the way to speedy disaster. There had been revolts before and they had always been quickly and savagely crushed. The leaven of Christianity had to work in the world for many generations before the abolition of slavery became a practical possibility.[35]

We should recall that it was Christianity that finally overcame the horrible slave labor in England and America. The Christian abolitionist William Wilberforce's tireless efforts in Britain ultimately led to the complete end of slavery in all of the British empire's possessions by 1840, making it the first modern country to outlaw slavery.[36] In the United States, Christians fought and died to end slavery, including the Presbyterian preacher Elijah Lovejoy (who was murdered for his fight against slavery), Edward Beecher, Lyman Beecher, Charles Torrey (the father of the

---

[33] Barclay, 211.

[34] Id.

[35] Barclay, 212-13.

[36] Alvin J. Schmidt, *Under the Influence: How Christianity Transformed Civilization* (Grand Rapids, MI: Zondervan, 2001), 278.

underground railroad), and Harriet Beecher Stowe.[37] Unfortunately, human trafficking and slavery persist in the United States and throughout the world, and Christians should be actively engaged to support ending human trafficking.

Most of us, however, do not live as slaves in our modern world, so how can we apply Peter's words in this passage to our daily lives? Maybe the closest parallel we have today is the relationship of employer-employee (don't you sometimes feel like your boss is a "slave driver"?) How can we apply what Peter says to slaves to our work situation? For one thing, if we do have a Christian boss, or even a kind and considerate boss, we should be careful not to abuse that kindness and take it for granted. Peter is probably addressing this type of situation. As Christianity spread, many freemen and slaves became Christians and thus "brothers" in the Lord. Often, in any given congregation, a slave could be a leader in a church. Callistus, one of the earliest bishops of Rome, was a slave. As Christianity spread, the social barriers of slavery began to come down. As this new situation emerged, what was the slave to do? If his master was a Christian, should the slave take advantage of that situation and not do the work his master wanted him to do?

Peter urges the slaves to consider themselves as "slaves of God." In the same way, Paul urged his readers to realize that they were not working for their masters, but rather for Jesus (Col. 3:23). How would your attitude at work change if you knew that everything you do was done for Jesus? Is Jesus satisfied with your attitude at work? "The Christian must be a better workman than anyone else. His Christianity is not a reason for claiming exemption from discipline; it should bring him under self-discipline and make him more conscientious than anyone else."[38] Much of our daily lives are spent at work, so work is the best opportunity we will often have to show others what God has done for us. Like Peter, we need to realize that our lives are so much deeper and fulfilling when we stop working to catch fish and start working to serve, love, and influence others.

---

[37] Id. 279-280

[38] Barclay, 212.

But what if I have a mean boss, a boss that mistreats me? Peter says that it is "commendable" (literally, it is "grace") if we "bear up" under that situation because we are "conscious" of God. To be "conscious" of God would mean to have an understanding of God. A true understanding of God when you are suffering unjust wrong is simply to recall how those who put their trust in God (and in particular, Jesus) were not disappointed. God is able to use even unjust suffering to bring about good things. The same word for "bear up" is the word that Peter will use in the next verse to describe how Jesus "bore" our sins in the most unjust suffering of all. Jesus is our example of how to deal with unjust suffering. In this verse, Peter makes the point that it is precisely in our suffering that we experience the "grace" of God in Jesus. We can experience God's grace if, during suffering, we recall that God suffered for us and along with us. We can experience God's grace if, during pain, we remember that our suffering will not be in vain, but we have the hope of the risen Jesus. That hope "does not disappoint us because God has poured out his love into our hearts by the Holy Spirit, whom he has given us" (Rom. 5:5). Jesus can meet us when we suffer, and he will come to our hearts because He too suffered unjustly.

Lord Jesus Christ, thank you for experiencing suffering for me. Thank you, Lord Jesus, that you suffered for me in taking away all my sin. Today, I may be faced with difficult people in my workplace. I may be mistreated. Instead of letting that create bitterness, help me to remember you died for them too. Release me from the bondage of bitterness. As you taught us to do, I pray for those in my life who have mistreated me. May I be an instrument of your peace to them. May they see You in me. In Jesus' name, Amen.

JESUS SHOWS US HOW TO SUFFER

²¹ To this you were called, because Christ suffered for you, leaving you an example, that you should follow in his steps.

²² "He committed no sin, and no deceit was found in his mouth."

²³ When they hurled their insults at him, he did not retaliate; when he suffered, he made no threats. Instead, he entrusted himself to him who judges justly. (2:21-23).

Jesus is our model for how to suffer. Peter goes so far as to say that we were "called" to suffering opportunities so that we might have the chance to imitate and become more like Jesus. Jesus suffered for us, leaving us an "example" that we should imitate him. The word for example, *hupogramos*, refers to the way a child was taught how to write in the ancient world. The term can mean either an outline sketch of something or the words at the top of a page that a child would copy when learning to write. Peter is saying that we learn the high art of Godly suffering by looking at how Jesus suffered.

What was the result of Jesus' suffering? God's love and grace spread throughout the world; whole cultures have been changed by the power of unselfish and unconditional love. Peter is saying that in the same way, our suffering can actually be a means for God's grace to impact others if we will entrust our suffering to God and "bear up" under it. He even points to specific things we should remember and do when we suffer:

1. *Remember, God suffered for you.* First and foremost, we must remember that God suffered, and he suffered for us. God is familiar with suffering—he experienced it as a Father losing his Son; he experienced in the flesh in the person of Jesus. All of his sufferings were for us because he loves us. God is not far from our pain; he understands and suffers with us.

2. *Don't complain to others, but cry out to God.* Jesus didn't make any threats, and he didn't tell lies about others. What he did is cry out to God, and that is certainly okay to do. God encourages us to offer our "laments" to him and cry out to him. The Psalms are filled with laments of suffering, godly people who cry out to God (see, in particular, Psalms 13, 22, 69, 74). We must take our grief and pour it out to God. He listens to us and can soothe and heal our broken spirits. He is the "Shepherd and Overseer" of our souls (1 Peter 2:25).

3. *Don't retaliate, but pray for those who mistreat you.* We must remember that God is the greatest avenger, and He says that "vengeance is mine, I will repay" (Deut. 32:35; Rom. 12:19). Trust in the wisdom and patience of God, because those who are intent on doing harm will fall into the pit they have dug for themselves: "The trouble he causes recoils on himself; his violence comes down on his own head" (Ps. 7:16). Revenge and bitterness only keep us captive and strangle us. Jesus taught us to bless those who persecute us and to pray for those who mistreat us (Luke 6:20). The only way that evil can overcome us is if we let it destroy us on the inside, and the only real way to overcome evil is to smother it with love.

4. *Entrust your suffering to God, "who judges justly."* That is what Jesus did. When he suffered on the cross, he surrendered his suffering to the Father, and what did God do with it? He redeemed the whole world with it. In the same way, good can come out of our suffering if we commit it to God and follow Jesus' example. Again, evil can only be overcome by

love. Paul encourages us: "Don't be overcome by evil but overcome evil with good" (Romans 12:21).

Peter is reminding us that if we give our suffering to God, then even our unjust suffering can be an opportunity for God's "grace" to shine. Such was the example of Korean Pastor Yangwon Son. In 1948, a band of Communists had executed Pastor Son's two older boys, Matthew and John. These boys died as martyrs, with their last breaths trying to persuade their persecutors to call on Jesus. Later, when the Communists were expelled, a young man in the village, Chaisun, was identified as one of the triggermen who killed Matthew and John. Chaisun was sentenced to execution, but Pastor Son and his daughter pleaded for mercy, and Pastor Son offered to adopt Chaisun. Such grace was overwhelming to Chaisun, and Chaisun experienced the grace of God and became a Christian.[39]

Father God and our Lord Jesus Christ, I commit my suffering to you today. I turn it over to you. I do not know what to do with it, and I do not see how this will all turn out. But I know you are strong enough to handle it. You are loving enough to receive it, for I remember how you suffered for me. You are powerful enough to weave it into something that will be beautiful someday, someway, in your time. Right now, I need your Presence, your closeness, Your Spirit. Comfort me, God of all comfort. Hold me. Reassure me. Let me feel your love. In the name of Jesus, Amen.

---

[39] Clowney, 113-114.

THE GOD WHO SUFFERS

24 "He himself bore our sins" in his body on the cross, so that we might die to sins and live for righteousness; "by his wounds you have been healed." 25 For "you were like sheep going astray," but now you have returned to the Shepherd and Overseer of your souls. (2:24, 25)

1 Peter is a book about suffering, and the God revealed in Jesus is a God acquainted with pain. As John Stott has said, "I could never myself believe in God if it were not for the cross. The only God I could believe in is the One Nietzsche ridiculed as 'God on the cross.'"[40] When it comes to understanding suffering, we have to go to the cross. The cross is the place where God meets us in our pain.

Much of human suffering has come about because of humanity's selfishness, brutality, and godlessness. The question "Why is there suffering in the world?" could easily be met with the questions "Why did the first person have to die?" and "Why does anyone have to die?" Theologically, the answer involves our own free choice. Because we have chosen to be our own gods, we have cut ourselves off from the source of Life itself, the God of all creation. But the Bible tells us that even before God created us, He had already dealt with our selfishness, brutality, wickedness, and

---

[40] John R. W. Stott, *The Cross of Christ* (Downers Grove, Il: Intervarsity Press, 1986), 335.

separation from Him. Peter has already said that Jesus was chosen before the foundation of the world to redeem us by his precious blood (1 Peter 1:20). In Jesus' sacrifice on the cross, God joins us in our suffering. Let us reflect on the suffering God went through in sending his Son to the cross.

The day when God banished man from His Presence, when His just verdict said "Death," His heart was crushed. He knew what this meant. He knew that *He* would have to bear the consequences. His love demanded it. In love, He had allowed man to make his own decision. Love demanded that. Love requires free choice; otherwise, it is not loving, and God is love. So love allowed (and allows) for the possibility of evil because of our freedom to choose. But love has even greater concerns than just free choice. The Father's concerns ran in two directions: preservation and redemption. As any good father must, He was concerned about upholding His universe. If God allowed it, the evil that humans have introduced would eventually contaminate, unravel, and destroy His universe. (What if Adolph Hitler were allowed to live and destroy forever? How horrible the thought!) But the Father had a more significant concern than simply preserving his universe: He was more concerned about rescuing humans. He was concerned about undoing the consequences of evil, to bring humans back to life! God must uphold justice and, at the same time, rescue humankind from the grip of evil. How does he do this?

In C.S. Lewis' *The Lion, the Witch, and the Wardrobe*, Aslan the Lion represents Jesus Christ, and in the story, Aslan's sacrifice points to God's answer: there is "Magic" that is deeper than evil, a Magic that runs from before time began. This Magic says that "when a willing victim who had committed no treachery was killed in a traitor's stead, the [Stone] Table would crack and Death itself would start working backward."[41] And so Aslan himself was offered on the very Stone Table that demanded justice. Lewis's story provides a picture of what happened in reality. Jesus, the innocent, offered himself on the very cross where we should all be. The only way to make it right was for God himself, the only innocent one and the Judge

---

[41] C. S. Lewis, *The Lion, the Witch, and the Wardrobe* (New York: HarperTrophy, 1994), 163.

of all, to bear the punishment; for God's only Son to bear the consequences in human flesh. And because He took the punishment, no one can accuse God of not being just; now, no one can blame us any longer for our failures. If God does not condemn us, who can?

In the cross, we see something worse than death--it is evil. But in the cross, we see there is something more powerful than evil--it is love. At the heart of the universe is a furious, blazing, holy Love that will stop at nothing to change His children. This Love has healed our souls by searching for us, calling for us, joining us in our pain, carrying us back in His arms, healing us from the terrible wounds of our sin. Like a Shepherd searching over every hill and valley for a senseless, lost sheep, God has entered humanity to search for you and me through the moments of our lives. If we catch a glimpse of that kind of Love, we will return with our hearts wide open and allow Him to oversee, protect, and rule our hearts forever.

Father, I am amazed that you are the kind of God you are. When I consider this universe, I am amazed at the enormity and complexity of it. But I know that this universe is not a cold, dead place. It is a vibrant, alive place, filled with your love. I have come to see this love through your Presence, and through Jesus Christ. Jesus died on the cross for me, and I understand that at the heart of the universe is your furious, blazing, Holy Love. Today, help me catch a glimpse of this kind of Love through the moments of my day. I turn my heart wide open to you and ask you to oversee, protect, and rule my heart today. In Jesus' name, Amen.

A BEAUTIFUL WIFE

¹ Wives, in the same way submit yourselves to your own husbands so that, if any of them do not believe the word, they may be won over without words by the behavior of their wives, 2 when they see the purity and reverence of your lives. 3 Your beauty should not come from outward adornment, such as elaborate hairstyles and the wearing of gold jewelry and fine clothes. 4 Rather, it should be that of your inner self, the unfading beauty of a gentle and quiet spirit, which is of great worth in God's sight. 5 For this is the way the holy women of the past who put their hope in God used to adorn themselves. They submitted themselves to their own husbands, 6 like Sarah, who obeyed Abraham and called him her lord. You are her daughters if you do what is right and do not give way to fear. (3:1-6)

Now we come to family relationships, the most important of all human relationships. Peter starts by saying "in the same way," a phrase which he had used when talking to slaves, but also a phrase he uses in 4:7 when talking to husbands. The point is not to say that wives should be submissive to their husbands in the same way as slaves to their masters, but Peter uses the phrase instead to tie the entire discussion about relationships together. There is continuity between all relationships; they all depend on mutual submission and respect.

Notice also that Peter does not say that women should be submissive to men, but only that a wife should submit "to her own husband." This is not a general instruction for all women to be submissive to men, but that each wife should be faithful in her marriage to her own husband. The Old Testament passage to which Peter alludes (i.e., Sarah calling Abraham her "lord") indicates that wives should be submissive and faithful in a sexual nature toward their husbands. The only recorded time when Sarah calls Abraham "My lord," is when she is told by an angel that she will bear him a son, and her response is "My lord is old!" (Gen. 18:12). Nevertheless, she submits to Abraham sexually in order to fulfill the promises of God. "Thus both in verse 1 and in verse 5 the meaning of the wife's submission to her husband concerns the sexual relationship and should not be taken in a more general and oppressive way."[42] This is the same thought Paul stresses in 1 Corinthians when he tells his readers that the husband's body is not his, but his wife's, and that the wife's body is not hers, but her husband's (1 Cor. 7:4).

Peter spends a lot of time talking to wives, and in particular he deals with the situation where a wife becomes a Christian but her husband remains a pagan. This was common in the early church and presented a delicate situation. In Roman, Greek and Jewish cultures, a wife was legally and culturally subject to the authority of her husband. Thus, if a man became a Christian, his wife would automatically also become one. But not so if the wife became a Christian first. That could easily upset the cultural norms and create friction in the family unless the wife acted like "Christ" toward her husband. This is what Peter urges his women readers to do: to live such attractive lives that their husbands are "won over without a word." The Greek word for "won over," *kerdainein*, is always used in the New Testament to refer to humility as an instrument of conversion.[43] Augustine mentions this same attitude of his mother, Monica, who's beautiful and reverent spirit finally won over her husband toward the end of her life.[44]

---

[42] Hillyer, 92.

[43] Id. 95.

[44] Saint Augustine, *Confessions* 9:19-22 (London: Penguin Books, 1961).

Peter specifically contrasts the external aspects of beauty, such as clothes, hair, perfume, and jewelry, with the things that make a woman beautiful to her husband: the "hidden person of the heart." What is the hidden person of your heart? It is incredible how loud your inner self can talk when you have a spirit that quietly trusts in God; when you serve rather than want to be served; when you trust in God rather than frantically seeking your own way; when you seek first to understand rather than be understood.

Peter refers to a "gentle" spirit, which is a spirit that does not insist on its own way. He also speaks of a "quiet" spirit, which literally means restful, calm, full of peace. What Peter is urging wives to do is what we should all do: to have the peaceful Presence of God so much in our souls that we are at peace with whatever happens in the situations around us. That sort of gentleness and quietness is so attractive to a frantic, selfish world. Peter says this kind of spirit is "unfading" or "imperishable." Nothing can withstand or outlast it. In particular, if a wife who is married to a non-Christian has any chance at a long-lasting relationship with her husband, it must be one anchored in the peace of Christ, which passes all understanding. Such women "put their trust in God" and "do not give way to fear."

Peter says this was the way women of the past put their trust in God. Peter may have been thinking of such godly women in the Old Testament as Deborah, Hannah, Esther, or Ruth. Alfred Edersheim notes a statement made by a Jewish woman to her daughter: "My child, stand before your husband and minister to him. If you act as his maiden, he will be your slave and honor you as his mistress. But if you exalt yourself against him, he will be your master, and you will become vile in his eyes, like one of the maidservants."[45]

Although Peter is writing to an audience comprised of Gentile as well as Jewish Christians, he calls such women "daughters" of Sarah. Just as all believing Gentiles are sons of Abraham by faith (Rom. 4:11-12), so Gentile women who put their trust in God may be called "daughters" of Sarah.

---

[45] Alfred Edersheim, *Sketches of Jewish Social Life in the Time of Christ* (London: Religious Tract Society, 1876), 140.

For wives: Father, as a wife, I pray that you will fill me with a gentle, quiet, confident spirit today. Let me listen to my husband. Let me honor him and make him feel special. I turn our relationship entirely over to you, knowing that as I trust in you, you can change the dynamics of relationships in ways I could not have imagined.

For husbands: Father, as a husband, I pray that I will draw out the hidden person of my wife. Let me listen to her. Let me honor her and make her feel special. Let me speak tenderly to her and understand what she is going through today. I turn our relationship entirely over to you, knowing that as I trust in you, you can change the dynamics of relationships in ways I could not have imagined.

We love you. In Jesus' name, Amen.

A LISTENING HUSBAND

⁷ Husbands, in the same way be considerate as you live with your wives, and treat them with respect as the weaker partner and as heirs with you of the gracious gift of life, so that nothing will hinder your prayers.(3:7)

It is hard for us to grasp how ground-breaking Peter's words were to the husbands of his day. In Greek, Roman, and Jewish culture, wives were the property of their husbands. The husband could be sexually promiscuous, but the wife could not; the husband could leave his wife, but it was difficult (and shameful) for a wife to divorce her husband. Peter is exploding this whole concept by calling wives the "partner" of her husband. Not only are wives urged to be faithful to their husbands, but the husband is now forbidden to be unfaithful to his wife. And what happens if a husband is not faithful? Peter makes it clear: God will not hear his prayers. That's a frightening thought.

While we should understand the impact that Peter's words had on his culture, we need to apply what he says to us today. Husbands, how is God telling you to treat your wife?

1. *Considerately.* Literally, this means that we should treat our wives "according to knowledge," in a way that takes "consideration" of her needs. Many husbands might be saying, "Who can understand women?"

Peter is not asking us to understand women; he is telling us to understand our wives. He is also not asking us to "read her mind." He is telling us to get to know her particular needs, wishes, goals, fears, and dreams. How do we do that? The best way is to ask. We should be in the habit of asking our wives: "Where are you at right now? What is bothering you today? What are you concerned about?" We also need to listen! Pay attention! How often do our wives drop us hints of how they are feeling, and yet we are more concerned about the game on TV or our own needs and we don't hear what she is trying to tell us.

2.   *Respectfully.* The word respect is not strong enough to express the Greek words used here (*aponemontes timen*). Literally, it means "preciousness." Our wives should be precious to us. We should treat them as having such value that we honor and respect them in every situation and at all times.

3.   *Tenderly.* Peter says that husbands are to treat their wives as, literally, the "fragile vessel." Peter is using a visual image to say that your wife is like beautiful china, intended to be treated special. Peter is referring to her physical strength when referring to here as "fragile," and not to her emotional strength. When it comes to fortitude, women are stronger than men. Yet women are more finely tuned and intricate. Just as a plastic cup is different from Watermark crystal, so is a woman different and intricate. Husbands, pray to God to understand how tender your wife's feelings are, and how much weight your words have with her. Don't be careless in what you say to her or how you treat her. Instead, treat her just as you would a delicate, expensive crystal.

4.   *Equally.* Peter says that our wives are "co-heirs" with us of the gracious gift of life. Malachi refers to the wife as her husband's "partner" (Malachi 2:14), and Paul says that in the Lord Jesus, "woman is not independent of man, nor is man independent of woman. For as woman came from man, so also man is born of woman. But everything comes from God" (1 Cor. 11:11-12). God has called husbands and wives to be "one flesh."

"One flesh" means that in every way, they are joined together and cannot operate apart from each other. Physically, the husband's body is his wife's, not his own. So he cannot do with it whatever he wants—his wife owns it equally. Concerning their children and their families, couples should be on the same page. They are partners in raising their children in the Lord. Socially and psychologically, they must be united and on the same page, partners working together. God has called husbands and wives to this level of unity, and only by His Spirit can that level of unity be attained and sustained. We must pray for God's Spirit to be the controlling influence in our marriages so that God can bring about that equality to which He calls us.

Peter concludes his discussion of husbands by saying that we should treat our wives in these ways "so that nothing will hinder your prayers." Peter is alluding to Malachi 2:13-16, in which the people of Israel complain that God no longer hears their prayers. Malachi gives them the reason God is not listening:

"*It is because the Lord is acting as the witness between you and the wife of your youth, because you have broken faith with her, though she is your partner, the wife of the marriage covenant*" (Malachi 2:13-15).

It is a dangerous thing not to treat our wives considerately, tenderly, and with respect. Conversely, we are the ones that are blessed when we do treat our wives considerately, tenderly, and with respect. As Paul said, "He who loves his wife loves himself" (Ephesians 5:28).

Father, as a husband, I pray that you give me a tender heart so that I can listen to and see the hidden person of my wife. Let me know what troubles and worries her. Let me listen not only to what she is saying today, but what she is not saying, how she feels, what her plans are, what her dreams are. You are my example, you who are such a great Husband to the church. Let me learn from Jesus how to live sacrificially, tenderly, actively, and confidently. May my wife know today through my words and how I treat her that she is loved, respected, honored, and my equal partner in life. Thank you for her. In Jesus' name, Amen.

A COMPASSIONATE COMMUNITY

⁸ Finally, all of you, be like-minded, be sympathetic, love one another, be compassionate and humble. 9 Do not repay evil with evil or insult with insult. On the contrary, repay evil with blessing, because to this you were called so that you may inherit a blessing. (3:8, 9)

The word "finally" makes us think Peter is wrapping up his letter, but he is only finishing his address to slaves, wives, and husbands. He has been speaking to each as a specific group, and now he addresses all of them together. In our culture today, it might be as if he were saying: "Now then, whether you are acting as an employee, a wife, or a husband, here is what you should do in all situations...." We should keep in mind that Peter's initial readers were experiencing suffering. Peter wants his readers to see that they can still be blessed, even while experiencing intense suffering, if they entrust themselves to God, just as Jesus did.

Peter says if Christians will entrust themselves to their Creator and take these specific actions, they will inherit a "blessing." The word "blessing" (*makaros*) is the same word Jesus used in the Sermon on the Mount ("Blessed are the poor in spirit, etc.). Peter mentions five action words, four of which are found only here in the New Testament. We can also tie these same actions back to Jesus' teachings (and blessings) in the Sermon on the Mount:

FROM FISH TO GLORY

1.   *We should have "one mind."* The word Peter uses, *homophrones*, is used only here in the New Testament and means "one mind." The thought is more than just unity; it implies that we all think alike. Is Peter calling for the impossible here? Even in a church, it is easy for Christians to have different agendas. Some may think we should focus more on benevolence; others may think we should put more emphasis on evangelism. Some may think we should spend more money on foreign missions; others may think we need to focus on our own neighborhoods. People are different, and all of us have differing gifts and differing ideas of how best to serve and worship God. So how can we have "one mind?" What would this "one mind" be? Paul tells us in Philippians 2 what kind of mind we should have: the same mind as Christ had. That mind is full of serving the needs of others and not thinking more highly of ourselves than we ought to. That type of mind has an attitude of self-emptying sacrifice, just like Jesus did when he gave up heaven and came to die for us on the cross. We should have one mind, and that should be a mind like Jesus. Remember, *"blessed are the peacemakers."*

2.   *We should be sympathetic.* Again, the word Peter uses is used only here in the New Testament. The word, *sympathies*, means "suffer with." The church is a unique place in the world where people are not too afraid or distant to suffer with each other. One of our problems as sinful people is that we don't want to get too close and let others know our faults, fears, and problems. Often, when someone joins a church it takes time for them to open up and let others into their lives. We are guarded. But whenever a problem occurs, and we turn it over to God and seek help from others, we can experience the real Presence of God's Spirit through the tender service of other Christians. We, as Christians, should "suffer with" others. Remember, *"blessed are the merciful."*

3.   *We should live as "loving brothers."* Again, the word Peter uses is found only here in the New Testament, and it is a beautiful word. It is the word *philadelphoi*, which means "brotherly love." A similar term, *philadelphia*, is used in 1:22. The force of this word is that we should have the same

affection for other Christians that we have for our biological brothers and sisters. How do we obtain that kind of love? It is an outgrowth of the love that God has for us. But it needs nurturing, and that can only come as we spend time ministering and sharing with other Christians. Our relationships with our Christian brothers and sisters are often deeper and more loving than relationships with our biological families, and such is what Jesus predicted: "Whoever does God's will is my brother and sister and mother" (Mark 3:35). Again, *"blessed are the merciful."*

4. *We should be compassionate.* The word Peter uses is a strong word. He is saying, literally, that we should "feel from our bowels" or from our internal organs. The English word "compassion" is the right term because it means "with passion." We should have a passion for the lives, hurts, fears, goals, dreams, and future of our Christian brothers and sisters. Again, this takes time and effort. Jesus calls us to move out of our comfort zones and have "passion" for the lives of others. Remember, *"blessed are those who mourn"* with others.

5. *We should be humble.* Peter again uses a word (*"tapeinophrones"*) that is used only here in the New Testament. Humility is always a mark of God's Presence. God opposes the proud but lifts up the humble. Humility is not always an admired trait in our world. The world often applauds self-assertive people. But Jesus says it is the "meek" who will inherit the earth. Humility and meekness should not be viewed as timidness or powerlessness, but rather as our energies submitted to the hand and will of God. You might say it is "strength under control" or strength channeled to serve others. Remember, *'blessed are the meek."*

As we have seen, Peter's words echo those of Jesus spoken in the Sermon on the Mount. Those who practice them are indeed "blessed." The Beatitudes would be helpful for us to commit to memory and meditate on during the day.

Father God and our Lord Jesus Christ, I am thankful for my brothers and sisters in Christ. How thankful I am for the close friends that I have. Let me be thankful today for my friends, and help me to be more "friendly" today. I gain so much in the body of Christ. May I be more sympathetic, humble, compassionate, and serving of my Christian friends today, so that the world may know that we are disciples of Jesus. In the name of Jesus, Amen.

HOW TO LOVE LIFE AND SEE GOOD DAYS

Do not repay evil with evil or insult with insult. On the contrary, repay evil with blessing, because to this you were called so that you may inherit a blessing. ¹⁰ For,

*"Whoever among you would love life
and see good days
must keep your tongue from evil
and your lips from deceitful speech.*

*¹¹ Turn from evil and do good;
seek peace and pursue it.*

*¹² For the eyes of the Lord are on the righteous
and his ears are attentive to their prayer,
but the face of the Lord is against those who do evil." (3:10-12)*

God calls us to turn our relationships "upside down." Usually, if we are treated badly, our natural response is to treat the other person the same way. But Jesus tells us to do just the opposite! "If someone strikes you on the cheek, offer him the other also. If someone takes your shirt, give him your coat as well" (Matt. 5:39, 40). Why? This is so counter to our natural inclinations. After all, shouldn't justice be done? Why do we do this? Jesus says we do this so that we might become more like the Father, "who sends the rain on the just and the unjust" (Matt. 5:45). In our human relationships, mercy should triumph over justice, just like it did on the cross. Don't they deserve our revenge? Yes, they do. But that is not the question we should ask.

The question we should ask is: *what would God do?* When someone cuts in front of you on the freeway, ask yourself: what would God do? When a business partner cheats you, ask yourself: what would God do? Peter doesn't say it will be easy, and the slap on the other cheek will probably sting. But it is this kind of suffering that God calls us to, unjust suffering, just like Jesus endured. Why? Peter says, "so that you will inherit a blessing." Again, the word for "blessing" is the same root word that Jesus used in the Sermon on the Mount to describe those who show the character traits of those God blesses.

And there is another reason: instead of two wrongs being committed, God will use our merciful actions to change the situation completely! This is the truth of the old Jewish proverb, which says that whenever we repay evil with good, we are "heaping burning coals upon our enemies head" (Prov. 25:21, 22; Rom. 12:20). In other words, our merciful action completely takes away the force of evil from the other person. They have no power over us when we forgive them and offer a healing response. Instead of further violence, such a merciful response humiliates the other person, hopefully causing them to repent. Meeting force with force only creates an explosion; meeting force with kindness takes the life out of the force. "Don't be overcome by evil, but overcome evil with good" (Romans 12:21).

Peter again quotes from his favorite Psalm, Psalm 34. This Psalm was a favorite for Jews under persecution, and Peter also applies it to his Christian readers who are undergoing suffering. The Psalm is a promise to all believers that God will give us good days, that he will watch over us, and that we shall see his face. This promise is particularly important in light of the suffering of Christians that Peter has just mentioned. If we trust God and return good for the evil that we experience, will God bless us?

The Psalm is sort of a riddle, with the question being: Do you want to enjoy life? Do you want to have real, enjoyable life that is satisfying in this life, but that extends forever? "Yes, yes!" you answer. "How?" The Psalm answers the riddle:

1. *Keep your tongue from evil and deceitful speech.* Jesus said that as the mouth speaks, so the heart thinks (Matt. 12:34). Jesus also tells us how we will be judged: *by our words!* (Matt. 12:37) The most destructive part of our bodies is our tongue (James 1:26; 3:1-12) because it causes more heartache than any other. The Bible is filled with admonitions to be careful what we say (see, for example, Prov. 10:11, 12:19, 13:3, 17:27, Eph. 4:25, 26, 29).

We would do well to pray before we say anything harsh, deceitful, in anger, or in any way manipulative. We should develop the habit of praying before we speak and before we hit the "send" button on our emails. We should be "quick to listen, slow to speak, and slow to become angry" (James 1:19).

2. *Turn from evil and do good.* The "blessed life" consists both of a turning from the things that destroy our lives and a pursuit of truth, joy, holiness, and life. Peter has already told us to rid ourselves of all malice, deceit, hypocrisy, and envy (1 Peter 2:1) and to crave the nourishment that God gives us so we may "grow up" (1 Peter 2:2). In the same way, Paul says to "put off" our old self, which is being corrupted by deceitful desires, to let God change the way we think by continually renewing our minds in His Word, and to "put on" the new self, created to be like God (Ephesians 4:22-24). We must "turn from evil and do good."

3. *Seek peace and pursue it.* How do you "seek peace"? How do you "pursue it?" Peace is something that we do not often see in our world. We are frantic people, "having an address but never at home."[46] We pursue peace in our souls by resting in God and finding time to be alone with Him. How

---

[46] Henri J.M. Nouwen, *Making All Things New: In Invitation to Spiritual Life* (San Francisco: Harper, 1987), 36.

do we pursue peace when we are in a hostile situation with others? It won't just happen: we have to do the hard work and make it happen by sacrificing our pride and seeking reconciliation. Paul told us that we should not worry about anything, but in everything, by prayer and petition, we should make our requests known to God, and the peace of God, which passes all understanding, will guard our hearts and minds in Jesus (Phil. 4:6.7). The early Christian writing, 2 Clement, encouraged Christians with this thought: "If we are zealous to do good, peace will pursue us" (2 Clement 10:2).

Peter concludes the quote from Psalm 34 by reminding us that the eyes of the Lord are on the righteous and his ears attentive to their prayers. As Psalm 34 stated, the Lord is "close to the brokenhearted" (Psalm 34:18). One of the most significant promises of the Bible is in 2 Chronicles 16:9, which says, "For the eyes of the Lord range throughout the earth to strengthen those whose hearts are fully committed to Him."

Father, today I will keep my tongue from deceitful and evil speech. I will start to do that by meditating on Your excellent Word. Let Your Word dwell within me richly. Today, I will turn from evil and do good. When the "bad" happens to me today, I will give it up to you. It is not within my power to turn evil into good, but it is your specialty to do that, so I will give you the evil, trust in You, and respond with that trust. Today, I will seek peace and pursue it. Not only will I seek that which makes for peace among my family, friends, and co-workers today, but I will seek Your peace throughout the day in meditating on You and Your Word. Keep me in perfect peace. Thank you. In Jesus' name, Amen.

WHAT TO DO WITH SUFFERING

¹³Who is going to harm you if you are eager to do good? 14But even if you should suffer for what is right, you are blessed. "Do not fear what they fear; do not be frightened." But in your hearts reverence Christ as Lord. (3:13,14)

Peter now moves to the central theme of the letter: What to do with suffering? He first asks the question: "Who will harm you if you are eager to do good?" You would think the answer would be "nobody." But in reality, we know that is not always the way life is. The question then is: How do we cope with unjust suffering? Sometimes it is easier to endure suffering if we can see a reason for it. Unjust suffering is difficult, however, because there seems to be no reason for it.

Peter has begun his answer to this question with the little Greek word "*ou*," which means "then." Peter is tying unjust suffering with his reference to the "eyes of the Lord" which he mentioned in verse 12. Peter is reminding us that since the eyes of the Lord are on the righteous and his ears are attentive to their every prayer, and since his face is against those who do evil, then who will dare harm you for doing good? Paul had said the same thing when he said, "If God is for us, who can be against us?" (Rom. 8:31). David had said, "In God I trust. What can mortal man do to me?" (Ps. 56:4) Peter is reminding us of what David concluded in Psalm 73: the end of the evil person always ends in death, and the judgment of God, though it may seem slow, is always sure.

Although God promises a final righting of the wrongs and eternal security with God, He never promised that life on earth would be trouble-free. Jesus reminded us that "in this life, you will have troubles" (John 16:37). Suffering is often the lot of Christians, as Paul bluntly put it in Philippians 1:29: "For it has been granted to you on behalf of Christ not only to believe on him but suffer for him." We may be ostracized and criticized by others just by living a good lifestyle, which may make them feel uncomfortable.

God never promised we wouldn't suffer, but he does give us these significant promises:

1. *Suffering won't last forever.* Peter says in 1 Peter 5:10 that after we have suffered "a little while," God will himself restore us and make us strong. The bedrock of our faith is the resurrection of Jesus from the dead. Without that living hope, we would, as Paul said, be of all people most pitied (1 Corinthians 15:19). But, Paul says, "Christ has indeed been raised from the dead," and our new life in Him after death is assured by His resurrection. Thus, we know that in the Lord, our labor is not in vain" (1 Corinthians 15: 58).

2. *God, the "with us God," will be with our spirits to help us endure and even redeem the suffering.* Jesus is our "Emmanuel," the "with-us God." God is not far away; He has come near and dwelt among us and experienced the same sufferings we experience. As the writer of Hebrews reminds us, "Because he himself suffered when he was tempted, he is able to help those who are being tempted" (Heb. 2:18). The writer of Hebrews goes on to remind us we can approach this kind of God because he understands suffering: "For we do not have a high priest who is unable to sympathize with our weaknesses, but we have one who has been tempted in every way, just as we are—yet was without sin. Let us then approach the throne of grace with confidence, so that we may receive mercy and find grace to help us in our time of need" (Heb. 5:15-16).

So what should we think when unjust suffering comes our way? Peter says we should consider ourselves "Blessed!" Yes, you heard it right: Blessed! Although this may seem strange, to consider suffering a blessing gives us a whole new outlook on suffering. As we pointed out in 1 Peter 3:8, the word Peter uses for blessing (*makaros*) is the same word Jesus used when he said, "Blessed are you when people insult you, persecute you, and falsely say all kinds of evil against you" (Matt. 5:11). The word for blessing means "divine generosity." In other words, we should see in our suffering how God can be generous in using our suffering for greater things.

How is it possible for God to use our suffering for greater things? For one thing, suffering purifies us; it galvanizes us and clarifies our priorities. Many things bring fear to our lives: losing our job, losing our spouse or our children. And yet, when suffering comes, we are forced to fling ourselves in complete trust to God. Where else can we go? When the things we thought were supporting us are kicked out from under us, we must fall into the waiting arms of God. When our fear becomes a reality (such as losing our job), we realize there is only One to fear, and yet in His hands, all fears are gone. He will sustain us, and we have, in the end, nothing to fear.

In her book on the tragic death of her husband, Todd Beamer, on September 11, 2001, Lisa Beamer writes:

> Probably the most important truth is that my security must be in God rather than in anything or anyone in this world…I have found safety and security in a loving heavenly Father, who cannot be shaken, who will never leave me or forsake me, and in whom I can trust completely. For those looking for hope, I recommend grabbing the hand of your heavenly Father as tightly as possible, like a little child does with his parent. God is a hero who will always be there when you need him.[47]

These are Peter's thoughts as he now quotes from Isaiah 8:12, "Do not fear what they fear; do not be frightened." The antidote to the fear of people

---

[47] Lisa Beamer and Ken Abraham, *Let's Roll: Ordinary People, Extraordinary Courage* (Wheaton, Il: Tyndale, 2002), 300-01.

is awareness of the power and nearness of Almighty God. It is helpful to understand the context of Isaiah 8:12. Isaiah is preaching to the people of Jerusalem around 735 B.C., a time when they faced not only the threat of invasion by the ruthless Assyrians but an imminent danger of attack by the kingdoms of Syria and northern Israel. Isaiah reminds them that they need not fear what men might do, but that "the Lord Almighty…is the one you are to fear, he is the one you are to dread, and he will be a sanctuary" (Isa. 8:13-14). God will be a "sanctuary" to those who wait and trust in Him. But those who do not trust in God will stumble, and God will be to them a "stone that causes them to stumble, and a rock to make them fall" (Isaiah 8:14). God even shows how near He is by giving them a sign. The sign was a child who would rule over David's throne (a Messianic promise), and who would be called "Wonderful Counselor, Mighty God, Everlasting Father, Prince of Peace" (Isaiah 9:8). Of course, this sign of God's nearness was ultimately fulfilled in the coming of Jesus, who is our sanctuary, our Rock, our Counselor, and the One who is able to give us peace if we trust in Him. So, instead of fearing those who might hurt us, we should "reverence Christ as Lord."

Father, I do not fear what the world fears. I have seen You work in situations that I thought were hopeless. I have experienced Your Presence through prayer, through Your Word, and through my friends who trust in You. I know You have even conquered death, so I am not afraid even of death. I know that suffering lasts only for a while, and You have proven through the suffering of Your Son Jesus that You are with me during my suffering. So, bless me today, even though I may suffer. Bless me through this suffering and confirm in my soul this blessing. In the name of Jesus, Amen.

SHARING YOUR HOPE

15But in your hearts set apart Christ as Lord. Always be prepared to give an answer to everyone who asks you to give the reason for the hope that you have. But do this with gentleness and respect, 16keeping a clear conscience, so that those who speak maliciously against your good behavior in Christ may be ashamed of their slander. 17It is better, if it is God's will, to suffer for doing good than for doing evil. 18For Christ died for sins once for all, the righteous for the unrighteous, to bring you to God. (3:15-18)

Right in the middle of talking about unjust suffering, Peter breaks into talking about being prepared to share your faith. Why is this? Because it is often in situations where we have to suffer that the world takes note of our lives and asks us: "How can you endure this? What makes you tick?" Peter might be thinking of a situation where a slave acted graciously to a harsh master, and by being gracious, won the respect of the master. In our case, it may mean being nice to a bad boss or being courteous to a rude customer or client, or simply smiling to the person who cut you off in traffic. Remember, people are always watching you, and particularly when hard times come your way.

Notice how Peter phrases his statement. He doesn't say: "Always be prepared to give the correct answers," or "Always be prepared to give a theological discourse on the existence of God, the incarnation of Jesus, the atonement, and heaven." No, he simply says, "Always be prepared to give an answer for the hope *you* have." We don't need to give people a long-winded analysis of our faith. If they want to sit down and discuss deeper issues, we can do that with them. But Peter is simply saying that we should share what Jesus has meant to us and what he has done in our lives. We may not know all the answers to all the questions people ask. That's okay. Only the Spirit can convict people's hearts and lead them to the truth (John 16:8-10). But we can tell them what God has done for us.

And we should do this with "gentleness and respect." An obnoxious Christian is a fake Christian. People should smell the aroma of Christ, not the stench of self-righteousness. Paul put it this way: "Let your conversation always be full of grace, seasoned with salt, that you may know how to answer anyone" (Col 4:6). The "salt" that Paul mentions is wisdom, gentle wisdom that attracts people and, just like salt, makes them thirsty for more. Peter is telling us to be gracious and respectful so that our life and our words will attract those around us.

Remember, your lifestyle speaks much louder than your words. That's why Peter tells us to "keep a clear conscience." People can spot a hypocrite a mile away. Unfortunately, one bad act can prevent someone from ever wanting to listen to us. As St. Francis is known to have said, "Preach the gospel, and if necessary, use words."

Just as people dismiss our message when we live hypocritical lives, so people are attracted to us when we respond graciously to unjust treatment. When someone treats us harshly or poorly, and we respond with grace and love, they are very much "shamed." It is at just such a time that their hearts can be convicted of the truth of God's love for them, and, as Peter says, they are ashamed of their slander. Peter again mentions that suffering in life can come to us because we deserve it (because of wrong or sinful decisions we have made), and suffering in life can come unjustly or because we are trying to do the right thing. When the latter happens, we should accept it as God's will and let God use and redeem that suffering. Our model for this is, of course, Jesus, who suffered more unjustly than anyone in human history. So, when people take advantage of us, or talk behind our back, or slander us, or offend us in any way, we must remember that it was for our sins that Jesus was treated in the same manner. He unjustly took all the blame for what I have done, the "righteous for the unrighteous." If he does that for me, I can certainly endure suffering caused by other people's unjust actions. I also must remember that because of Jesus' unfair suffering, I was brought to God. The love shown in his suffering attracted me to God and has saved my life. God used that suffering for great and positive things. In the same way, I must remember that God will redeem and use the unjust suffering I endure. No suffering is wasted when given into the hands of God.

Father, make me aware of the people around me today. Help me to see their hurts and their needs, just like You do. When you present the right time, strengthen me to give the reason for why I hope in You. Help me to do it with gentleness and respect, just like Jesus did. And if things don't go my way today, remind me that people are looking at me, and they will notice how I respond. So keep me in your perfect peace today. Thank you for being with me. In Jesus' name, Amen.

JESUS THE VICTOR

He was put to death in the body but made alive by the Spirit, [19] through whom also he went and preached to the spirits in prison [20] who disobeyed long ago when God waited patiently in the days of Noah while the ark was being built. In it only a few people, eight in all, were saved through water, [21] and this water symbolizes baptism that now saves you also—not the removal of dirt from the body but the pledge of a good conscience toward God. It saves you by the resurrection of Jesus Christ, [22] who has gone into heaven and is at God's right hand—with angels, authorities and powers in submission to him. (3:18-22)

We come to a difficult passage to understand. Martin Luther commented that this was "a more obscure passage perhaps than any other in the New Testament, so I do not know for a certainty just what Peter means."[48] We should have the same humility as we consider it.

A few preliminary thoughts might help us in considering this passage. First, anytime we try to interpret a Biblical text, we need to consider the context of the passage. Peter has been talking throughout his letter about facing unjust suffering and even death, and he has been encouraging Christians to entrust themselves to God, who will redeem their suffering.

---

[48] Hillyer 113.

Verse 18 has explicitly spoken about the triumph of Jesus' suffering, and how that suffering brought us to God and how Jesus was made "alive in the Spirit" (meaning he was raised from the dead). This context "sets the scene for verses 19-22, which describe the extent of that triumph."[49] Since in Jesus' risen body death has been conquered, Jesus is free to do his work in the spiritual realm. The history of civilization since the resurrection of Jesus is a testimony to the power of Jesus' work after his resurrection.

Second, we should keep in mind that Peter is probably using concepts about the dead that appeared in the literature written between the time of the Old and New Testaments (the "Apocryphal" literature), with which his readers would have been more familiar. For example, when Peter refers to the "spirits in prison who disobeyed long ago when God waited patiently in the days of Noah," he may be referring to the fallen angels mentioned in Gen. 6:1-4. This would be in line with the popular traditions in Jewish literature in the intertestimental period. These fallen angels were said to be representatives of evil kings on the earth: "This judgment wherewith the angels are judged is a testimony for the kings and mighty ones who possess the earth" (1 *Enoch* 67:12). Or Peter could be referring to the generation of people who lived during the days of Noah, whom Judaism considered the worst generation that ever lived and who could never be saved: "The generation of the Flood have no share in the world to come" (*Sanhedrin* 10.3).

So let's now analyze each statement that Peter makes and consider possible interpretations. First, Peter says that Jesus was made alive in the Spirit "through whom" he went and preached "to the spirits in prison." What does "through whom" (*en ho*) mean? Peter seems to be saying that Jesus is acting either "in or through the Holy Spirit" or in a "spiritual state" when he went and preached to the spirits. The idea is that Jesus was liberated from bodily death and now reigns and acts in the "spiritual" realm. This should give Peter's readers great encouragement because they are not facing their persecution alone: Jesus, in the spiritual realm, is certainly with them.

---

[49] Id.

Second, when did he go and preach to the "spirits in prison?" We cannot say for sure, but it would appear from the context to be either between the time of his death and his resurrection, or after his ascension. In either case, the thought is that Jesus is alive and active in the spiritual realm. The idea that Jesus was active in some way between his death and resurrection is hinted at in Matthew 12:40, Acts 2:25-27, 13:35, Romans 10:7, Ephesians 4:9, and Revelation 1:18.

Third, what did Jesus preach to these spirits in prison? Did he preach an offer of salvation or an announcement of judgment? The most likely answer is that it was a message of both judgment and salvation. Judgment and salvation are always tied together in Scripture. One cannot accept salvation unless one realizes the judgment of God on his life. Thus, if judgment is intended here, Peter could be saying that Jesus is proclaiming in the spiritual realm that the power of evil has been completely demolished (see Paul's similar statement in Colossian 2:15). This would have bolstered the confidence of Peter's readers who were facing evil persecution. However, we must also remember that salvation is the theme of the Bible and it is God's love that ultimately overcomes evil. Although the Greek term used here (*keryssein*) is a neutral term meaning any public announcement, in the New Testament is it always used to refer to the proclamation of the good news. Furthermore, 1 Peter 4:6 indicates that it was the "good news" that was preached to the dead: "For this is the reason the gospel was preached even to those who are now dead, so that they might be judged according to men in regard to the body, but live according to God in regard to the spirit."

Fourth, just who are these "spirits in prison" to whom Jesus preached? If they refer to the fallen angels who are represented by evil rulers on earth, then Peter could be encouraging his readers to follow Jesus' example and boldly proclaim the good news to the pagan rulers. If they refer to the most evil generation for whom there is no chance of salvation, then this would be an example of God's incredible love to preach salvation even to the worst of sinners (examples of which, by the way, the Bible is replete). If so, then Peter's readers would be encouraged to preach to the heathen culture that surrounded them. These "spirits" could also refer to all of the wicked that preceded Jesus (i.e., the Old Testament dead). The early church understood this passage as indicating that Jesus, between his death and resurrection, went and preached to all those who had died before (see, for example, Tertullian, *On the Soul*, 55). In the ancient world, Sheol or Hades was considered the place of the dead, and the place of the dead was often considered a "prison house," applied to both humans and fallen angels (see Rev. 18:2; 20:1-7; 2 Peter 2:17; Jude 6; 1 Enoch 10:4-5).

Peter's use of the generation of Noah allows him to make a perfect application of what happened in Noah's day to his readers. Peter in effect uses Noah to illustrate God's active salvation in his (and in our) day. First, Noah was surrounded by wicked people, and yet God waited patiently and was able to rescue and save Noah and bring about God's plan of salvation. Second, throughout history the majority of people have rejected God, but God has still been able to rescue a "remnant." Thus, in Noah's day, only 8 people in all were saved. The application to Peter's readers (and to us) is that we should not be discouraged that the culture around us for the most part rejects God and godly ways. Third, just as Noah was saved from the wickedness around him and water was involved in his deliverance, so Christians are saved and baptism is a symbol (the Greek word is "*antity-pon*," or "antitype") of how Noah was saved. The word "antitype" means that the flood was a figure that had its ultimate fulfillment in the work of Jesus which we accept in baptism. Just as God saved Noah from the wicked culture around him "through" the flood, so God saves us "through" our baptism.

Peter is quick to point out that it is not the baptism itself which saves us, but the grace and power of God. It is not the physical act of baptism itself which saves us—that would simply be a "removal of dirt from the body." Instead, baptism needs to be seen as a "pledge of a good conscience to God," and we need to remember that the saving comes because of the "resurrection of Jesus Christ." What does Peter mean when he says baptism is a "pledge of a good conscience to God?" The word for "pledge" (*epero-tema*) actually means "question," and probably refers to the question asked of a baptismal candidate as to his belief and commitment to Jesus.

Peter concludes his thoughts by reminding us that Jesus has ascended to heaven and that all powers and authorities are in submission to him (see also Matthew 28:18). Thus, although we live in a society bent on destruction, Jesus has already won the victory over evil and death, and God's purposes ultimately will prevail.

Father, I do not understand all the mysteries of this universe, but I have come to know Your heart. I can trust You because Your ways are true to reality and Your love is never-ending. Thank you for reminding me that there is such a thing as judgment, and I am grateful for your judgment on my life. If you were to allow me to continue in my ways, I would end up completely destroying myself. But you judged me to wake me up! And at the same time you judged me, you saved me by taking completely that judgment upon yourself. What an incredible God you are! Praise Your Name! Thank you, in the name of Jesus, Amen.

THE BLESSINGS OF SUFFERING

¹Therefore, since Christ suffered in his body, arm yourselves also with the same attitude, because he who has suffered in his body is done with sin. 2As a result, he does not live the rest of his earthly life for evil human desires, but rather for the will of God. (4:1,2)

In these verses, Peter focuses on one of the blessings that comes from suffering: it can purify us and prioritize our lives. Peter puts it bluntly: the one who suffers in his body is "done with sin." Wouldn't you like to be "done with sin?" Wouldn't you like to stop fighting that persistent habit, whether anger, worrying, chemical dependency, lust, or whatever? Unfortunately, while we are in this body, we will never be free from *temptations* to sin. Temptations will always be there. But the urges to sin will, and should, decrease the closer we grow to God. Suffering has a way of purifying us. How does suffering do this?

1. *We are humbled in suffering.* Suffering humbles us, and in the process, much of our natural pride is stripped from us. That humility opens the space for God to come into our souls on a deeper level, and through suffering, we can experience the reality of God and deepen our dependence on him.

2.   *Suffering makes us more sensitive to the hurts and needs of others.* Until we truly suffer, we may not have much of a compassionate spirit. Suffering can make us empathetic and sensitive to others. We are keen to the needs of others because we have also felt pain and need. This, in turn, releases us from selfishness and makes us more willing to help and love others.

3.   *Suffering focuses our attention on what is important in life.* When we suffer, our concerns about minor things suddenly are dropped. We begin to take a "long view" of life. We ask questions such as: "What am I doing with my life? Is it worth it?" If you knew you had only a year to live, would that change the way you live now? Of course it would. Suffering teaches a person to "not live the rest of his earthly life for evil human desires, but rather for the will of God" (verse 2). Suffering teaches us to learn to live for what God's will is, to take a long view of life.

As always, our model on how to endure suffering is Jesus. Jesus suffered for something he did not do. His betrayal, trial, scourging, and crucifixion were all unjust and senseless. Jesus experienced, with excruciating physical and emotional pain, unjust and senseless suffering.

How in the world did he endure such unjust and senseless suffering? Peter answered that question in 1 Peter 3:18: "For Christ died for sins once for all, the righteous for the unrighteous, to bring you to God." How did he do it? He realized in his suffering that it would "bring *you* to God." Jesus was able to endure suffering because he was thinking about *you.* He knew that his suffering would bring you to God, and he knew that it was the only way to bring you to God. The writer of Hebrews says that it was for the "joy set before him" that he endured the suffering (Heb. 12:2). The joy Jesus had on the cross came from seeing the smile on your face when you realized how much God loves you, and seeing your life transformed by His Spirit.

Similarly, our suffering can be endured when we realize that someone can benefit from our suffering. In this way, suffering can be *redemptive.* God can "redeem" all our suffering, even what seems senseless, and make it useful and worthy. Martin Luther King, Jr. endured much unjust suffering as he struggled for the freedom and rights of others. He writes:

My personal trials have taught me the value of unmerited suffering. As my sufferings mounted I soon realized that there were two ways in which I could respond to my situation--either to react with bitterness or seek to transform the suffering into a creative force. I decided to follow the latter course. Recognizing the necessity for suffering, I have tried to make it a virtue. I have lived the last few years with the conviction that unjust suffering is redemptive.... There are those who will find the cross a stumbling block, others consider it foolishness, but I am more convinced than ever before that it is the power of God unto social and individual salvation. So like the Apostle Paul I can now humbly, yet proudly, say: "I bear on my body the marks of the Lord Jesus."[50]

Henri Nouwen makes the wonderful statement that "Just as Jesus was identified by his wounds, so are we."[51] Nouwen reminds us that after he was raised, Jesus still had his wounds, which he showed to his disciples. Through these wounds, Jesus still identifies with those who hurt. This suffering love of God is part of what makes God so glorious: "The resurrection had not taken his wounds away, but, rather, they had become part of his glory."[52] The wounds Jesus still bears are a constant reminder to us of how God can redeem suffering. In the same way, Nouwen says, "our wounds are much more than roadblocks on our way to God. They show us our own unique way to follow the suffering Christ, and they are destined to become glorified in our resurrected life."[53] This means listening to our wounds "as teachers who help me find my own way to holiness, sharing them as a source of consolation and comfort, and allowing others to pour oil on them and bind them in times of great pain."[54]

---

[50] Martin Luther King, Jr., *Strength to Love* (Philadelphia: Fortress Press, 1963), 152-153.

[51] Henri J.M. Nouwen, *Seeds of Hope* (New York: Doubleday, 1997), 182.

[52] Id.

[53] Id.

[54] Id.

Father, thank you for reminding me today that suffering can have a purifying effect on me, but only if I turn it over to You. Help me not be bitter today about my suffering, but instead, show me how You plan to redeem it. I offer myself to you today so that you can redeem my suffering and turn it into something glorifying. Begin by using it to purify me so that I cling totally to you. Use it to humble me, to make me sensitive to others, to focus on what is really important during my time on this earth. I know that I shall live with You forever in glory without this suffering. But now, redeem it and use it to your glory. I commit this to you in Jesus name, Amen.

IT IS TIME TO MOVE ON

³For you have spent enough time in the past doing what pagans choose to do—living in debauchery, lust, drunkenness, orgies, carousing and detestable idolatry. 4They think it strange that you do not plunge with them into the same flood of dissipation, and they heap abuse on you. 5But they will have to give account to him who is ready to judge the living and the dead. 6For this is the reason the gospel was preached even to those who are now dead, so that they might be judged according to men in regard to the body, but live according to God in regard to the spirit. (4:3-6)

We get a sense of the suffering that Peter's readers were going through from this passage. They were surrounded by a culture intoxicated by sex, violence, and alcohol. Sounds a lot like our culture, doesn't it? To make matters worse, some of these Christians had formerly been caught up in that culture, and now their friends and associates were heaping abuse on them for not "plunging" into their sins. You can just imagine some of the comments: "Oh, so you're too good for us now? What makes you so holy? Do you think you are better than us?"

Maybe you have heard these same kinds of comments. When we try to live like Jesus, we will endure some sort of ridicule or persecution (Phil. 1:29). People simply do not like being judged, and if our holy lives make them feel uncomfortable, they will ridicule us to make themselves feel better.

So how do we deal with these situations? Peter reminds us again to take a "long view" of life. At the end of their lives, what are they going to show for it? Peter says that people who live for the moment "plunge" into a "flood of dissipation." What does that mean? "Dissipation" is a broad word that simply means *waste*. Peter is saying that people tend to jump into a *flood of waste*. Whenever we live for the moment, simply to please ourselves, we will find that we are wasting our time, our energy, our talents, our resources. That's really what sin is: one big waste of ourselves! Instead of going on a journey in life, we tend to get stuck on a merry-go-round, living for the day. Our culture caters to immediate pleasure, just like Peter's culture did. Everywhere we turn, we see advertisers telling us to "go for it" and satisfy our urges.

When we live selfishly, short-sighted lives, we end up misusing our energies and talents. Instead of using our talents, time, and resources for good things that lead to a long and joyous life, we cheapen our lives. So much talent has been wasted by lives caught in the traps of addiction.

In the end, what will we show for our lives? What will people say at our funeral? What will be inscribed on our tombstone? Even more, what if there really is a life after death—what then? Peter reminds us that all of us will have to meet the One who created us. We all will have to give an account to "him who is ready to judge the living and the dead" (verse 5). As the Psalmist said, we must remember to "number our days" that we may "gain a heart of wisdom" (Psalms 90:12), and as Paul said, we should "be careful how you live, not as unwise but as wise, making the most of every opportunity" (Eph. 5:15).

Father, I have spent enough time living without purpose. I pray that today you will channel my life for Your greater purposes. As I look around at the world today, it does look like a flood of waste. My heart goes out to those consumed by the lie of wealth, by chemical addiction, by a lack of love. If someone today criticizes me for trying to live dedicated to You, then let me return that with Your love. I know that is what they desperately need, so let me be ready today. Thank you for giving me overwhelming love and purpose. I commit my way to you today. I love you. In Jesus' name, Amen.

LIVING WITH THE END IN MIND

⁷The end of all things is near. Therefore be clear-minded and self-controlled so that you can pray. (4:7)

Peter reminds us that "the end of all things is near," meaning not so much the end of time, but the end of our days on this earth. Peter has already told us that "All men are like grass, and all their glory is like the flowers of the field," which is here today and gone tomorrow (1 Peter 1:24, 25). He now brings three related thoughts together: (i) live with the end in mind: (ii) be clear-minded and self-controlled; and (iii) pray. These three things are interrelated. When we live with the end in mind, we are more focused on what is important. By staying focused on what is important, we can have more control over ourselves. The word for "clear-minded" Peter uses is *sophronein*, which could be translated "keep your sanity by being wise." We live in an "insane" world, with demands and pressures bombarding us every day. How do we keep our sanity? By living wisely and with perspective, by living with the "end in mind." The one thing that will help us live sanely, wisely, and with the end in mind is *prayer*.

Prayer, which is an *active communication life with God*, is at the root of all our spiritual growth because, in prayer, we invite God into all of our lives, and we encounter His Presence. We cannot have "self-control" unless God is the One controlling us. God can only control us as we submit ourselves to him. We do this chiefly by prayer. We give Him all of our fears. As Peter says, we "cast all our anxieties on Him" because he cares for us (1 Peter 5:7). We give him all of our failures. We give him all our future. We "practice the Presence" of God. Brother Lawrence, in his classic devotional book *The Practice of the Presence of God*, writes "in the beginning, a persistent effort is needed to form the habit of continually talking to God and to refer all we do to Him, but that after a little care His love brings us to it without difficulty."[55] The first benefit of the soul that practices the Presence of God is "that faith becomes more alive and more active in every occasion of our life."[56]

Peter mentions the word "prayer" only two other times in this letter. The first time he directs his words to husbands, telling them that they should treat their wives with respect and gentleness "so that nothing will hinder your prayers" (3:7). The point is that praying to God is related to how we treat others. Prayer changes how we treat others, and how we treat others affects our prayers. In this passage, Peter is making a similar connection: Keep the end in mind and be sober, so that your prayers will be effective. And the reverse is true: Pray, so that you can keep the end in mind and be sober.

The second time Peter mentions prayer is in 1 Peter 3:12, where he quotes Psalm 34, stating, "The eyes of the Lord are on the righteous and his ears attentive to their prayer." Peter is reminding us that God's "ears" are straining to hear our smallest prayers. We cannot face the daily grind or sufferings that come in this life without relying on Him in prayer. As Jesus modeled for us, we should "commit ourselves to our faithful Creator and continue to do good" (4:19).

Father, this day I rest in Your Presence and take the time to be still and rest in You. I move under Your protection and love, and that gives me confidence and security. Help me to keep the end in mind.

---

[55] Brother Lawrence of the Resurrection, *The Practice of the Presence of God* (New York: Doubleday, 1977), 28.

[56] Ibid, 99.

Help me to realize that life is much more than the "things" I try to accumulate, but that real life comes in giving and in being used for greater glory. In Jesus name, Amen.

LOVE DEEPLY

⁸Above all, love each other deeply, because love covers over a multitude of sins. ⁹Offer hospitality to one another without grumbling. ¹⁰Each one should use whatever gift he has received to serve others, faithfully administering God's grace in its various forms. ¹¹If anyone speaks, he should do it as one speaking the very words of God. If anyone serves, he should do it with the strength God provides, so that in all things God may be praised through Jesus Christ. To him be the glory and the power forever and ever. Amen. (4:8-11)

Peter gives us further insight into obtaining self-control and keeping our sanity: loving others. When we are actively seeking the best for the people around us (whether our family, co-workers, fellow students, or people in our community), we develop a more "selfless" state of mind. Ironically, becoming more self "less" makes us have more control over our selves. We were made to live in community. We need others. Giving ourselves to others keeps us sane, empowers our prayer life, and develops wisdom.

Peter uses a strong word to describe how we should love one another. The word translated "deeply" actually means "be stretched." The picture is of an athlete stretching as he runs. Peter says, "stretch yourselves for each other." If you have to go out of your way a little for others, that is good. If you are not "stretching" for others, you are not really using your spiritual muscles, and your "self-less" state of mind will not grow. One way to stretch yourself is simply by offering hospitality, by doing something nice for someone else without their even asking for it. When is the last time you opened your home for others? When is the last time you did something for someone else that "stretched" you a little? Love is a muscle; it will not grow unless it is stretched.

Peter says we should love because love "covers a multitude of sins." What does he mean by this? He could be alluding to Proverbs 10:12, where the thought is that "love overlooks offenses." Forgiving others is one way we should "stretch ourselves" for others. Peter could also mean that when we love others and stretch ourselves for others, God will overlook a multitude of our sins. But this sounds too much like Peter is saying that we would somehow earn our forgiveness by our good deeds, which is contrary to the gospel and God's unmerited grace. We must remember God is the One who "stretched" himself on the cross to forgive us of our sins when we didn't deserve His love. Peter could simply be saying that love, God's love for us, and God's love in us to empower us, is the only way we can truly live in community. By stretching ourselves in the same manner as Jesus did, His love spreads, and the world is able to see His love.

Peter gives us further practical ways to "stretch" ourselves in love: We should use the "gifts" God has given us. What is a "gift?" It may be a talent, but it is more than that. A gift is whatever way we can be of service to others; whatever way we can show love to others. Spiritual gifts are not gifts unless we give them away in service to others. You may be a talented speaker, but you do not have the spiritual gift of speaking unless you allow God to speak through you to edify others. Each of us has been given spiritual gifts as God's Spirit has determined (1 Corinthians 12:11). The gifts we have are God-given (we can take no credit for it), and they are not gifts unless we use them in service to others. Our job is to be faithful in using them in the manner God desires. Peter mentions particular types of gifts, but this list is not exhaustive. The two gifts he mentions are: speaking and serving. The gift of speaking is not just public speaking. Any speaking we do can be a channel for God's words. Every day we all have the opportunity to speak God's words to others. Likewise, serving doesn't mean serving in some official capacity. Every day we will have a chance to serve others. So, Peter is addressing all of us because we can all experience the "gift" God has given us to speak His words and to serve others. By giving in these ways, we are the ones receiving a blessing. This is God's "gift" to us.

Father, help me to "stretch" today in love, just like You stretched your hands out on the cross for me. Help me to use the gifts you have given me and thereby receive the greatest gifts from You. I love You. In the name of the One Who stretched out for me, Amen.

PARTICIPATING IN
JESUS' SUFFERINGS

¹²Dear friends, do not be surprised at the painful trial you are suffering, as though something strange were happening to you. ¹³But rejoice that you participate in the sufferings of Christ, so that you may be overjoyed when his glory is revealed. ¹⁴If you are insulted because of the name of Christ, you are blessed, for the Spirit of glory and of God rests on you.¹⁵ If you suffer, it should not be as a murderer or thief or any other kind of criminal, or even as a meddler.¹⁶ However, if you suffer as a Christian, do not be ashamed, but praise God that you bear that name. ¹⁷For it is time for judgment to begin with the family of God; and if it begins with us, what will the outcome be for those who do not obey the gospel of God? ¹⁸And,
"If it is hard for the righteous to be saved,
what will become of the ungodly and the sinner?" (quoting from Malachi 3:1-3) ¹⁹ So then, those who suffer according to God's will should commit themselves to their faithful Creator and continue to do good. (4:12-19)

Peter returns again to the topic of suffering, and this time it seems clear he is talking about the persecution of Christians. In the early church, even before the official persecution of Christians by the Roman empire, Christians were often persecuted by the culture. Christians were seen as

atheistic (because they did not believe in the Roman gods), as unpatri-
otic (because they did not bow to the Roman Emperor), and as cannibals
(because they participated in the Lord's Supper). The Romans did not
understand Christians and often made fun of them. As early as the first
century, Christians were often excluded from business guilds and shunned
by society. As Christianity spread, Rome began to view Christianity as a
threat to its stability. With the rise of Caesar worship, Christians were sys-
tematically persecuted in the second and third centuries.[57]

Unfortunately, in our Western society today, there is a stigma associated with being a Christian. Christians are wrongly depicted in the
media as uneducated, "fundamentalists," weird, behind the times, and
prejudiced. While our society preaches tolerance of all faiths, it does not
want Christians to say anything about their faith. In Muslim countries, it
is much worse: Christians are slaughtered or jailed for their beliefs. Peter
reminds us all: Don't be surprised. Jesus promised that we would be persecuted because we follow Him (John 15:20). But Jesus also promised that
the Holy Spirit would be with us in times of persecution (Mark 13:1). Peter
calls this type of persecution a *pyrosis*, which means a refining by fire. Peter
had already compared suffering to a refiners fire in 1 Peter 1:7 when he said
that "all kinds of trials" have come so that our faith may be "proved genuine" in the same way that gold is refined by fire. The result of this suffering
will be "praise, glory, and honor" when Jesus is revealed to the whole world
(1:7). A refiner's fire is scorching and dangerous and can destroy things
put into it. However, as Timothy Keller states, "if used properly, it does
not destroy. Things put into the furnace properly can be shaped, refined,
purified, and even beautified. This is a remarkable view of suffering, that
if faced and endured with faith, it can in the end make us better, stronger,
and more filled with greatness and joy. Suffering, then, actually can use evil
against itself."[58]

---

[57] Clyde L. Manshreck, *A History of Christianity in the World* (Englewood Cliffs, NJ: Prentice-Hall, 1985), 22.

[58] Timothy Keller, *Walking with God Through Pain and Suffering* (New York: Dutton), 8.

One of the most important things to remember when we suffer is that God suffers with us, or, as Peter says, the "Spirit of glory and of God rests on you" (vs. 14). The Greek word for rest, *anapauetai*, is an allusion to the *Shekinah*, or the Presence, of God in the temple, which appeared as a thick, bright cloud that filled the temple with the glory and Presence of the Almighty (Exod. 40:34-35; 1 Kings 8:11). This same Spirit of glory rests on us when we undergo suffering. Hillyer points out that the Presence of God is promised by Jesus in times of persecution (see Matthew 10:20; Mark 13:11; Luke 12:11-12; John 14:26).[59] One beautiful example of God being with those in the refiner's fire is the story of Shadrach, Meshach, and Abednego in Daniel 3. These young men did not worship the idol of King Nebuchadnezzar but entrusted themselves to God's protection. When they were thrown into the fiery furnace as punishment, they were not destroyed, but God himself was with them in the fire! The king's men yelled, "Look! I see four men walking around in the fire, unbound and unharmed, and the fourth looks like the son of the gods" (Daniel 3:25). Isaiah might have had this scene in mind when he tells the people of Judah what God says: "When you pass through the waters, I will be with you; and when you pass through the rivers, they will not sweep over you. When you walk through the fire, you will not be burned; the flames will not set you ablaze….Do not be afraid, for I am with you" (Isaiah 43:2, 5).

In sum, Peter says that when suffering comes, we should do the following:

1. *Don't be surprised.* Jesus said in this world, we will have trouble, but we should not fear because Jesus said: "I have overcome the world" (John 16:33). We should not be surprised if we are persecuted for being Christians. Remember, we are in good company (Jesus said the great prophets of old were persecuted). We should also remember how God provided for those who trusted in Him, and we should especially remember the outcome of Jesus' life. God can turn any crucifixion into a resurrection.

---

[59] Hillyer, 135.

2. *Rejoice that you "participate in the sufferings of Christ."* How do we participate in the sufferings of Christ? Howard I. Marshall reflects, "Part of the mystery of evil is that it cannot be wiped out but only overcome by the suffering love of God incarnate in Christ....When we suffer, it is not a sign of God's lack of love or concern for us."[60] Rather, when we suffer, we have the opportunity to be used by God to overcome evil, both in our lives and in the lives of those around us.

3. *Don't be ashamed.* Suffering certainly humbles us and knocks us to our knees. But we have nothing to be ashamed of in our suffering. Sometimes we do suffer because we are experiencing the consequences of our sin. Still, even in those situations, we must remember that Jesus has completely taken away our sin and guilt, and there is no condemnation for those who trust in Him (Romans 8:1). God is able to take even our worst sins and use them to His glory. But much of our suffering is not caused by our sins, but rather is senseless and unfair. In those types of sufferings, we must not think that God is punishing us. As Jesus told his disciples in John 9, it is not because the blind man or his parents sinned that he was born blind, but that the glory of God might be revealed and that Jesus may be recognized as the sight-giver He is. We have one more reason for not being ashamed: God suffers with us. Jesus himself died a criminal's death on the cross. As Tim Keller states, "We do not know the reason God allows evil and suffering to continue, or why it is so random, but now at least we know what the reason is not. It cannot be that he does not love us."[61] With God suffering with us, we cannot be ashamed.

4. *Commit yourself to a faithful God and continue to do good.* When we suffer, we have to actively and consciously commit our hurting, bitterness, and fears to God. Keller reminds us that "Peter is saying that the fiery furnace does not automatically make us better. We must recognize,

---

[60] I. Howard Marshall, *1 Peter,* IVPNTC (Downers Grove, Ill.: InterVarsity Press, 1991), 157.

[61] Keller 121.

depend on, speak with, and believe in God while in the fire. God himself says in Isaiah 43 that he will be *with* us, walking beside us in the fire."[62]

Faithful Father and fellow sufferer Lord Jesus, You are to be praised not only for overcoming death and the worst that could happen to us, but also for walking with us through our suffering and redeeming the evil in the world. We hold Your hand today, and we place ourselves under Your protective care. Help me today to commit myself to You and continue to act in obedience to You in every way. I love you. In Jesus' name, Amen.

---

[62] 229.

TO THE ELDERS: SHEPHERD!

¹To the elders among you, I appeal as a fellow elder, a witness of Christ's sufferings and one who also will share in the glory to be revealed: ²Be shepherds of God's flock that is under your care, serving as overseers—not because you must, but because you are willing, as God wants you to be; not greedy for money, but eager to serve; ³not lording it over those entrusted to you, but being examples to the flock. ⁴And when the Chief Shepherd appears, you will receive the crown of glory that will never fade away. ⁵Young men, in the same way be submissive to those who are older. (5:1-5)

Peter now turns to practical things as he begins to close his letter. His first word of closing exhortation is to the leaders in these churches, and in so doing, he is stressing the critical role of leaders. "As the leaders go, so goes the people." In the church, the primary force of leadership is the elders. As the early church grew, it adopted from the Jewish synagogues the idea of a council or group of elders. Paul urged Titus to establish elders in the Cretian churches (Titus 1:5). Peter was an "elder," for here he appeals to these churches as a "fellow elder," one familiar with the issues confronting elders. We are reminded of Jesus' words to Peter in John 21:15-19, where Jesus reaffirms Peter (after Peter had denied him 3 times). Three times Jesus had asked Peter whether Peter "loved" him, and after every response from Peter, Jesus told Peter to do something for others: "Feed my lambs;"

"Take care of my sheep;" and "Feed my sheep." We show our love for Jesus by serving others, and leaders have a severe responsibility to nurture, protect, and guide those under their care.

Peter associates his serving as an elder with the fact that he is a "witness of Christ's *sufferings*." This statement is interesting because one would expect Peter to say: "as a witness of Christ's *resurrection*." Peter associates the role of leadership not with victory, but with the suffering of Christ. Peter has been telling the churches that Jesus is our "model" of suffering, and now he speaks to those who should take the lead in suffering. This exhortation reminds us that being an elder is not an office to showcase oneself, but a position of service in which the elder leads his flock in suffering and suffers with them, just like Jesus. An elder that suffers with the people in the church is consistent with the analogy of a "shepherd" because shepherds suffered for their sheep.

We are not familiar with shepherds in the Western world, but the concepts of an elder as a "shepherd" and the church as "sheep" are fitting. Just naming a few characteristics of sheep and shepherds will help us see how relevant these concepts are. As I mention each attribute below, try replacing the word "sheep" with "people" and the word "shepherds" with "elders":

- Sheep are dumb and stubborn. Shepherds need patience.

- Sheep are helpless and defenseless. Shepherds need to be "strong and courageous," as God urged Joshua (Joshua 1:6, 7, 9).

- Sheep have no idea what is best for them. Thus, a shepherd needs a lot of wisdom and needs to be continually seeking counsel and wisdom so that he can guide the sheep.

- Sheep are fearful creatures but respond to the voice of one who cares for them. That's why a shepherd "knows his sheep by name," and develops a tender relationship with each of his sheep.

- Sheep need constant care, and shepherds often get little rest and sleep. Thus, it is always a good idea for shepherds to take some time off and get some rest and re-charging so that they can best lead the sheep. Jesus recommended this (Mark 6:31).

Peter mentions some things that elders need to remember.

1.   Elders must remember that the church is not "their" flock, it is "God's" flock. Try as we might, we cannot force people to do as we wish; we can only seek to bring them to God and do all we can to help them grow into a stronger relationship with Him.

2.   Elders must remember to always examine their motives for leading. Don't be an elder out of a sense of "duty," but do it willingly. Don't be an elder for money or to bolster your ego, but serve "eagerly." You might say it should be done "full out" with all your heart, which is a demanding and challenging task. At times, elders and their spouses might be physically, emotionally, and spiritually drained. At such times they must ask God for a willing spirit; they must remember all that God has done for them; they must remember Jesus, who for the joy set before him endured the cross; and most significantly, they must remember that God is their Shepherd, and that when all seems dark and hard, He is able to lead us to green pastures and to restore our souls (Psalm 23).

3.   Elders must remember that the best way to lead is by example. Peter urges them not to "lord it over those entrusted to you," but serve by example. An elder cannot be on an ego trip; he must see each person in the church as one whose soul God has placed under his care. That is a heavy burden and requires that the focus always be on the souls in the church and never on the elder. Thus, the elder takes the lead in showing, by example, self-less love as he cares more about the spiritual growth of those under his care than he does about any recognition or applause.

4. Finally, elders must remember that the ultimate responsibility for their flock lies not with them but with the Chief Shepherd, who will someday reward the elder for faithful service. Spiritual leaders do not ultimately serve the church; they serve the Lord Jesus. Spiritual leaders do not serve or cater to culture or the selfish whims of those under their care; they serve the Lord Jesus. The goal of an elder is not success by the world's standards; the goal of an elder is to be faithful on a day to day basis.

Peter rounds out this discussion of elders by encouraging the "younger men" to be submissive to those who are older. In the context of this passage, it would appear that he is encouraging the "younger" elders to be submissive to the older ones and not to let their leadership position go to their heads. Submission and humility are good things for all of us as Christians to experience and accept. In this way, we are opening ourselves up to the character-building work of God and modeling our lives after Jesus himself. Peter turns to humility in the verses that follow, encouraging all of us to be humble.

Faithful Father, selfless Jesus, encouraging Spirit, be praised! Thank you that you are our Good Shepherd, Who knows exactly where to lead us to find refreshment to our souls and nourishment for our hearts. Thank you, Good Shepherd, for laying down Your life for me. Thank you also for the privilege of letting me be a partner with you in serving others. Teach me how to serve and how to lead by serving. Give me a renewed spirit today to feel the burden of those in my life who need Your touch. Thank you in the name of Jesus, my Good Shepherd. Amen.

GOD GIVES GRACE TO
THE HUMBLE

⁵All of you, clothe yourselves with humility toward one another, because,
"God opposes the proud but gives grace to the humble." ⁶Humble your-
selves, therefore, under God's mighty hand, that he may lift you up in due
time. ⁷Cast all your anxiety on him because he cares for you. (5:5,6)

Peter has been addressing elders and has encouraged the younger elders to
be submissive to the older ones. Now he encourages everyone, elders, and
flock alike to "clothe" ourselves with humility. The Greek word for clothe
(*enkomboomai*) occurs only here in the New Testament, and it refers to
a garment tied over outer clothing, like a slave's apron. Peter is no doubt
thinking about the slave's towel that Jesus put on the night before his crucifixion when he washed Peter's dirty feet (John 13). On that night, Jesus had
told his disciples that they would be "blessed" if they followed his example.
Peter had learned through the years that Jesus was right—that it is more
blessed to give than receive (Acts 20:35). Peter quotes from Proverbs 3:34
to stress the point: "God opposes the proud but gives grace to the humble."

In the next few verses, Peter lays out what true humility looks like
and how blessed we will be when we serve others in humility. First of all,
humility is essentially an *attitude* that is always thinking about how others
might be feeling or reacting. Humility is an active attitude of focusing on

others instead of ourselves. Humility is not an attitude of "I'm no good." That sort of defeatism has nothing to do with the Kingdom of God. When we think "I'm no good," we not only deny who we are in the sight of God, but the focus continues to be on ourselves instead of on others. We put on humility and serve others from an attitude of strength, not of weakness. We are all royalty and should always consider ourselves as the elect and special sons and daughters of God. When Jesus washed his disciple's feet, he did it out of a position of strength, not weakness. John tells us in John 13:3 that "Jesus knew that the Father had put all things under his power and that he had come from God and was returning to God." From that attitude of full confidence in God, Jesus put on the apron of a slave and washed Peter's feet. Jesus didn't have to prove himself in any way—He was already loved and accepted by the Father. Thus, Jesus could serve in the most hideous way, because He knew that God would take care of him and would multiply blessings out of his service. The reason that we are often not humble is that we feel that we have to prove ourselves. Instead of acting from a position of strength (like Jesus), we operate from a feeling of inadequacy and weakness. We don't want to be the first to say "I'm sorry" because the other person might see us as weak or take advantage of us. Only when we realize that God "opposes the proud but gives grace to the humble" can we make the first move and act out of humility.

When we realize that it is God who is watching and will take care of us, we can be the first ones to do the lowly, humble, even degrading thing. To drive this point home, Peter reminds us that we are not so much humbling ourselves before others as we are humbling ourselves before the "mighty hand of God." When I am the first to reach out and act, I am not so much doing this to the other person who has offended me as I am doing it to and for my God, who will take care of me.

We must also remember to stay on God's time. Peter reminds us that "in due time," God will lift us up. The New Testament uses two different words for time: *chronos*, which means chronological time (or clock time), and *kairos*, which has the sense of "the right time" or the "time of fulfillment." Peter uses *kairos* here, helping us remember that God will, when the time is just right, lift us up and exalt us. God's timing in the Bible and in history has always been just right, and since he is above time, he can lift us up at just the right time.

Finally, we must also remember to "cast all anxieties" on him, because "he cares" for us. The Greek term for anxiety means being pulled in different directions, which is exactly what happens when we worry. But when we trust ourselves to God's care, knowing he will, in due time, lift us up, we can endure a humiliating situation and humble ourselves before others. God will lift us up and give us grace, just as He triumphantly did in Jesus. Jesus is the shining example of what God will do when one completely trusts himself into God's hands.

Remember, humility is not a false sense of deprecation. We act from a position of strength, not weakness. Humility is an active service in response to how much God has given us and out of thankfulness for what He has done and continues to do in our lives.

Father, thank you for reminding me that true glory is found only in You and as I humble myself in Your Presence. "When a man thinks much of the glory of heaven, and little of his own glory, both the glory of heaven and his own glory are magnified. If, however, a man thinks little of the glory of heaven and much of his own glory, the glory of heaven remains unimpaired, but his own glory wanes." (Midrash Rabbah 4.20 on Num. 4:1). Help me to stay focused on your glory today. In Jesus' name, Amen.

RESIST THE ENEMY,
AND HE WILL FLEE

⁷Cast all your anxiety on him because he cares for you. ⁸Be self-controlled and alert. Your enemy the devil prowls around like a roaring lion looking for someone to devour. ⁹Resist him, standing firm in the faith, because you know that your brothers throughout the world are undergoing the same kind of sufferings. (5:7-9)

Peter pulls no punches in this passage. He wants us to see that life is a battle, and we are dealing with an "enemy" that wants to "devour" us. The New Testament warns us that we are dealing not just with physical enemies here in this world. We are engaged in spiritual warfare, both within our minds and within our culture. Paul warns us of this in Ephesians 6:12, reminding us that "our struggle is not against flesh and blood, but against the rulers, against the authorities, against the powers of this dark world and against the spiritual forces of evil in the heavenly realms." Peter calls this enemy the "devil," a term that conveys the same concept as an enemy: it means one who is an "adversary." Peter also calls him a "roaring lion" who "devours" his prey. In the natural world, a lion will use different methods to overcome his prey. Sometimes he will roar to paralyze his prey. Other times he will stalk his prey silently and will roar after he has attacked to scare away other predators.

In the same way, the devil is a master of evil. Sometimes he will para-lyze us with fear and anxiety. Sometimes he will wait until we are away from the strength and encouragement of our brothers and sisters in Christ. But Peter reminds us that the devil is not all-powerful, and he can be overcome and resisted. The devil can be overcome, and the Christian life should be a journey of spiritual growth in which our character is becoming more and more like Jesus. James 4:7 says that when we resist the devil, he will flee from us. So how can we overcome our enemy, the devil?

First, we cannot take him for granted, but we must be on the alert. We cannot just "drift" through life spiritually, for if we do, we will surely be attacked. Peter warns us to be "sober" and "alert." Peter probably remem-bers Jesus' words to him in the Garden of Gethsemane, when Jesus told him to "watch and pray" so that he wouldn't fall into temptation (Mark 14:38). We know that while the spirit is willing, the flesh is weak. Every day we need to be ready for battle, and as Paul warns us in Ephesians 6, every day we must put on the full armor of God so that "when the day of evil comes, you may be able to stand your ground, and after you have done everything, to stand" (Eph. 6:13).

Second, we must remember that sin grows out of our fear and anx-iety. We seek to escape from what makes us anxious, and we run right into destructive behavior. Usually, we give in to temptation when we want to relieve our anxiety or fulfill a craving by something other than what is good for us (and ultimately, the only good thing for us is God and his good gifts). In Psalm 139:23, 24, David ties these two ideas of anxiety and sin together when he says, "Search me, O God, and know my heart; test me and know my anxious thoughts. See if there is any offensive way in me, and lead me in the way everlasting." When we are anxious and worried, we have a "divided" soul and are easy prey for the enemy. That is why Peter men-tions in this passage that we must "cast" (literally, *throw, give up, get rid of*) all of our anxieties on God, who cares for each of us personally. When we throw our fears onto Him in prayer and let him take care of them, we are no longer divided in our souls. He picks up our cares and souls and unites our souls to him, and we become focused on him. The only way we can defeat the devil's schemes is by uniting our hearts to God in love.

Third, we must remember that a lion will not attack sheep when they stay together in the fold. But a sheep that is outside the fold is easy prey. In the same way, when we isolate ourselves from other Christians, we are asking for trouble. Merely attending church services on Sunday morning is not enough. God has designed the Christian church as an intimate, inter-active, organic body in which its members are vitally and closely connected to each other. Sin grows and breeds in darkness, and its power cannot be resisted when it is hidden. But sin's power and the devil's power vanish when sin is brought out into the light and seen for what it is—empty and destructive. We must confess our sins to each other and lean entirely on each other every day. Peter reminds these churches that they are not alone, but that their brothers throughout the world are engaged in the same struggle. Don't fight your spiritual battles alone because you cannot do it. However, as we team with one another, the devil can be resisted.

Finally, the devil attacks us when we are proud. As soon as we think we have overcome a particular sin and don't need God's help anymore, we fail. However, when we humble ourselves before God, the devil is resisted. Peter began this entire passage with the exhortation to clothe ourselves in humility. This whole passage is similar to James 4:7-10, in which James encourages us to "resist" the devil, and he will flee from us. James then tells us how to do this: draw near to God and humble ourselves in his sight. A humble person who leans completely on God will be able to resist the devil because God will be his strength. We cannot overcome the devil on our power. If we try, we will surely fail. The devil is conquered only in Jesus Christ. That is why Peter and James urge us to humble ourselves, which is why Peter tells us to "stand firm in the faith." Paul likewise tells us in Ephesians 6:13, 14 that after we have done all that we can to prepare, the most important thing is "to "stand." What does "to stand" mean? It means to stand within and under God's power. We don't try to "prove" ourselves spiritually. We just stand under God's protective care, casting all our anxieties on Him, humbling ourselves in his sight, enjoying his love and fellowship. When we are "standing under" God and "standing with" his people, the devil will flee.

Father, thank you that you are so powerful in every way. Lord Jesus, you are Lord of the universe, and all power and authority have been given to you. Thank you, Jesus, that you have come to destroy the works of the devil. Help me to realize that the devil steals, kills, and destroys, but that you bring life and life to the full! I will not drift through life, for I realize I am easy prey if I do. Help me today to stand in humility under your protective power. Let me not be anxious about anything, but in everything, I give all my anxious cares to you, because you care about me. Thank you that I need not fear, but resting in your strength can overcome the evil one. In Jesus' name, Amen.

SUFFERING IS TEMPORARY

¹⁰And the God of all grace, who called you to his eternal glory in Christ, after you have suffered a little while, will himself restore you and make you strong, firm and steadfast. ¹¹To him be the power forever and ever. Amen. (5:10, 11)

A significant theme throughout Peter's letter has been suffering. Peter has mentioned how suffering purifies and refines us. He has described how we can experience joy in suffering because, in our suffering, we feel the very Presence of God. When we suffer, we are merely following the example of Jesus, our model for suffering. Because Jesus is our model for suffering, any kind of suffering can be used to help other people and make us more sensitive to other people. When people see our suffering, they become changed, and thus God uses that for his glory. In that way, God can "redeem" our suffering, and we find we are "co-sufferers" with Jesus. But one thing we must always remember about suffering: it is *temporary*. Peter ends his letter by affirming that God provides grace to us in our suffering and that suffering is only temporary. Peter says that God is the "God of all grace." The thought here is that God can supply all the grace that we need in just the right way we need it. We remember how Peter described this grace as "many-colored" in 4:10. Peter had also described the suffering that we endure as "many-colored" in 1:4, with the thought that whatever color our suffering might be, God's grace will match it and prove perfectly able to shield and help.

Many stories in the Bible remind us that for those who suffered, their suffering was temporary, and God ultimately used their suffering in glorious ways. Let me name a few people whose suffering God ultimately turned into victory: Abraham and Sarah, who went childless for decades, but who finally had a son through whom Jesus' ancestry is traced; Joseph, who, as a teenager, was sold into slavery by his own brothers, but whose pain God worked for the good; Moses, who had to flee Egypt because of his own failings, but whom God used as an older man to rescue the people of Israel; Job, who endured unimaginable suffering, but whom God blessed even more after his suffering than he was originally blessed (Job 42:10); Paul, whose thorn in the flesh God used for his greater glory; and of course, Jesus, whose crucifixion brings salvation to all humanity and which God turned into a resurrection. The Old Testament story of Naomi is another beautiful picture of how God can turn suffering into something glorious. Naomi had lost her husband and two sons when they lived in the foreign country of Moab. When she returned home with only her daughter-in-law Ruth, Naomi told the people in Bethlehem not to call her Naomi anymore, but to call her "Mara," which means bitter (Ruth 1:20). And yet God, in his own time, blessed Naomi and brought Boaz, the "kinsman-redeemer," to Ruth. Ruth conceived and gave birth to Obed, the grandfather of King David and an ancestor of our Lord Jesus. After much suffering, Naomi could say that God had not stopped showing kindness to the living and the dead (Ruth 2:20).

Father God, I thank you that You hold all things together, and you hold me together when I suffer. I know that this life is not all there is, but that someday, You will wipe every tear from our eyes and will provide to us a new and glorious body. I know that even in this life, You have an incredible way of turning suffering into glory. Remind me today that suffering is only temporary. There will be a day when suffering is no more. My soul needs that reassurance. Only in the risen Jesus can any of us on this earth have any hope. But we do have hope, the living hope that is in Jesus. Thank you, my Jesus and Lord, and thank you my loving Father. In Jesus' name, Amen.

PARTING WORDS

¹²With the help of Silas, whom I regard as a faithful brother, I have written to you briefly, encouraging you and testifying that this is the true grace of God. Stand fast in it. ¹³She who is in Babylon, chosen together with you, sends you her greetings, and so does my son Mark. ¹⁴Greet one another with a kiss of love. Peace to all of you who are in Christ. (5:12-14)

We may have here the identity of the person who actually "penned" this first letter of Peter: Silas. It was common practice in those days for the writer of a letter to dictate his message to an "amanuensis" (a sort of scribe) and then for the writer to actually take the pen and write the final greeting (Paul did this in Galatians 6:11). This may have happened here, although we don't exactly know what Peter meant when he says he wrote this letter "with the help of Silas" (it is possible that Silas was the deliverer of the letter). Another rendering of the name Silas in this verse is Silvanus, the name Paul uses for this same person (see 1 Thess. 1:1; 2 Thess. 1:1; 2 Cor. 1:19). This person is probably the same one referred to often in Acts (his name appears several times in Acts 15-18). In AD 48, Silas was sent by the church in Jerusalem (of which Peter was a leading figure) to tell the believers in Antioch of the results of the Jerusalem settlement between Jewish and Gentile Christians, and he was the same person who accompanied Paul on his journey to Asia Minor and Greece (Acts 15:40). Silas is also named a co-author of 1 and 2 Thessalonians, and thus he may have possessed writing skills that both Paul and Peter utilized. If Silas assisted Peter in the actual writing of 1 Peter, then that might explain why 1 Peter's grammar and vocabulary appear to be so different from 2 Peter.

Peter says he has written briefly (105 verses!), but there is so much more he could have said. But what he has written was intended to be an encouraging word from his personal experience, "testifying that this is the true grace of God." Imagine in your mind the scene as Peter himself writes these last few words. Here is Peter, an elderly man, taking the pen in his hand and trying with his own handwriting to convey that God had been faithful and loyal to him in his life, that the grace of God had been tested through many failures and sufferings, and that this grace is the ultimate truth. And so he encourages them to "stand fast in it!"

Peter has been writing to the "*diaspora*," the exiles scattered about in Asia Minor. He now sends greetings from someone else in exile, "she who is in Babylon." Babylon was a code name for Rome (see Rev. 14:8), but Peter doesn't appear to be trying to hide the fact that he is writing from Rome. Instead, by using the term "Babylon," he is wanting his readers to know that he, too, is in exile, for Babylon was synonymous with exile ever since the Jews were first sent there in exile in 587 BC. The term "she" probably refers to the church in Rome because Peter says that she is "chosen together" with the churches to whom he is writing (the church is referred to in the feminine in 2 John 1, 13).

Peter also says that his "son" Mark also sends greetings. This person is probably John Mark, who had accompanied Paul on his first missionary journey (Acts 12:12, 13:5), and whom Paul mentions as a companion of his (Col. 4:10; 2 Tim. 4:11; Philemon 24). The term "son" probably does not connote blood relation but is instead a term of endearment, and it may refer to the spiritual mentoring role that Peter had with Mark. The early church believed that Mark was the author of the Gospel of Mark (which would have been the first gospel in chronological time) and that Mark wrote his gospel based on Peter's recollections while Mark was with Peter in Rome.

Peter ends by urging his readers to give one another a "kiss of love." The early Christians were known for their love for each other, and they would often give one another a "holy kiss" (see Rom. 16:16; 1 Cor. 16:20; 2 Cor. 13:12; 1 Thess. 5:26). The early Christians would embrace each other during their worship services, reflecting the deep love they had for one another. Unfortunately, this beautiful practice was replaced through the years with less physical signs of affection. The church, through the years, moved from kissing each other on the cheek to kissing each other's hands, to kissing only the priests' hands, and then to not hugging each other at all but kissing relics and furniture inside the church building! The church is a haven for Christians to experience the love of God and each other, and the church should restore the practice of hearty and loving embraces.

Peter has one last word for these churches and all of us: Peace. Peter could be saying, "May God's peace be with you," or he may be making the declaration that God's peace is with them. In either case, the promise to us all is not that we won't have tribulation in this world, but that Jesus has "overcome the world" (John 16:33). Thus, as Paul said in Philippians 4:7, even though we go through suffering, we can have the peace beyond understanding, a supernatural peace that comes from God and gives our hearts assurance of His Presence. These are the final words in this first letter from one of Jesus' best earthly friends, a person who had been through much suffering and could say with confidence at the end of his life that only God can provide that kind of peace.

Father God and Jesus, the Prince of Peace, thank you for these words from your servant Peter. Thank you that these Scriptures have Your very breath, and they can give me a new attitude about life, about suffering, about glory. Thank you that you are always faithful to your servants, and you always work together for good those you call. Thank you for the hope of glory, a living hope that comes alive every day. I love you and thank you. In Jesus' name, Amen.